COMBAT INVESTOR

T0147796

COMBAT INVESTOR

REAL ESTATE INVESTMENT WARFARE GUIDE

JOHN OHARENKO

authorHOUSE®

AuthorHouse™ LLC
1663 Liberty Drive
Bloomington, IN 47403
www.authorhouse.com
Phone: 1-800-839-8640

Published by AuthorHouse   08/10/2013

ISBN: 978-1-4918-0306-6 (sc)
ISBN: 978-1-4918-0305-9 (hc)
ISBN: 978-1-4918-0307-3 (e)

Library of Congress Control Number: 2013913990

This book is printed on acid-free paper.

Please visit: www.combatinvestor.com

DEDICATIONS

"Freedom is not free."
—Anonymous

This book is dedicated to all men and women of our armed forces. These people are the ultimate investors in America's real estate, risking their lives for us so that we enjoy all that this great country has to offer.

Thank you. We proudly salute you!

TABLE OF CONTENTS

PREFACE

It all started in the hood. Chicago's Humboldt Park neighborhood in the 1950s was the tempestuous site of my real estate investing boot camp. About three miles west of downtown, Humboldt Park is one of the most diverse communities in the nation—the best and the worst of America melts in this pot. An immigrant gateway since the 1860s, Humboldt Park has absorbed both the most productive, and the most dangerous German, Norwegian, Italian, Jewish, Polish, Ukrainian, African-American, Mexican, and Puerto Rican populations. It's home to many famous (and infamous) celebrities, including Saul Bellow, Mike Royko, "Baby Face" Nelson, Knute Rockne, and Coach "Mike" Krzyzewski.

Humboldt Park remains a real estate battlefield today—diverse, dangerous and exciting. Block to block, the area contrasts sharply between rows of beautiful nineteenth century greystones and gang-infested war zones. Real estate "turf" is marked by graffiti and historical landmark signs. Besides the residents, real estate "investors" include youth gangs, civic and religious leaders, and neighborhood protection associations. Walking two blocks in any direction is like crossing borders of several countries. Or war zones. Exciting, diverse, and dangerous.

My Ukrainian immigrant parents moved to Humboldt Park for the ample job opportunities and the ethnic comfort zone it so graciously offered. Since both of them worked, my after-school hours were supervised by a retired neighbor or "baba-sitter." I routinely slipped away with my friends to watch *Three Stooges* reruns, or, better yet, fool around out in the alley, or as we called it, Alley World.

Alley World. Chicago sports the largest network of alleys in America. A scenic prairie of garages with urban wildlife including alley cats, scrambling squirrels, fearless rats, free-roaming dogs, and still twitching road kill. A sports arena for pinners (a Chicago-style baseball game involving pitching a ball into a wall serving in place of a batter), pitching pennies, dodge ball, basketball, and field hockey played with rubber balls. Alley World was a year-round paradise. Summers we'd pop open a fire hydrant for an instant waterpark, and winters we'd bum a "ski ride" by grabbing onto a passing car's bumpers. Setting off fireworks (and sometimes even gunfire) had us running through backyards from neighbors, through gangways from cops—perpetual guerrilla warfare.

Alley World was our real estate empire to control, if only in spurts. As "the Earl of the Alley," "the Duke of Driveway," and "King of Concrete," I learned that real estate was just a fancy term for turf; and finding circuitous routes to a hideout where I could avoid a fist in the face was "investment strategy." I painstakingly pursued the dubious rank of tough guy and applied my urban stealth to avoid detection by my baba-sitter until it was time to head home for supper.

My parents soon realized the baba-sitter routine wasn't working. They yanked me out of Alley World and delivered me into what felt like a different planet—a suburban, Catholic military school. I found myself in a strange place with wide streets and endless cars (but no alleys!) that forced me to rethink my definition of both "turf" and "tough." Here, I pursued rank through promotions and medals. "Making it" in the streets required only to dare; "making it" in military school demanded strict discipline and supervised regimen. By the time I graduated, the tough guy in me brandished a brand new weapon—disciplined focus.

During summer vacations, my dad kept me away from Alley World by taking me along on his citywide sales trips, introducing me to the turf of the business world. I soaked it all in, and my "boots on the ground" experience soon turned me into a Chicago neighborhoods trivia expert.

Street savvy merged with textbook theory at DePaul University, where professors introduced me to terms like "real estate tax base" and "gentrification." These weren't just terms on the black board to me—they were descriptions of the turf I knew and loved! My real estate finance and investing studies were fueled by an assiduous work ethic instilled in me by University of Wisconsin Professor James "Chief" Graaskamp, a quadriplegic whose incarnation of tough put us all to shame. (I have never complained about the weight of any workload since!)

Once my recreation venue shifted from gang turf to sports, I began to notice uncanny parallels. Warfare, gang strife, sports—these were all expressions of our instinctive drive toward territorial expansion. Controlling the court, gaining yardage, stealing bases were all manifestations of force used to win, to protect oneself and to control one's space. The Hapkido studio soon became my new physical and psychological boot camp, and the black belt it earned me proved an invaluable and sacred combat investor tool for life.

When I started my career as a mortgage banker, my urban instincts were refined by financial savvy. The "tough guy in the streets" merged with the professional investor in the office and a combat investor was born. Through perpetual attitude adjustments, the combat investor in me has made work more satisfying, productive, and lucrative. Since 1980 I have weathered many real estate cycles, including double-digit interest rates, inflation/stagflation, Reaganomics, government bailouts of the savings and loans, the Japanese realty invasion, Internet, securitization and real estate bubbles, and the Great Recession. Still, I enjoy fighting on the front lines.

Despite plenty of mishaps and missed opportunities in my formative years, I've stood my ground—my battleground—for several decades, not because I studied wealth-building formulas but because I am constantly honing my attitude, sharpening my blade every day. I am always striving to be a "land mind."

In these pages, I share my "attitude artillery" in hopes that you too will unearth your war chest of realty riches. May *Combat Investor* arm you to, as Henry David Thoreau put it, "Go confidently in the direction of your dreams."

INTRODUCTION

Abracadabra, Hocus-Pocus, and *Mumbo Jumbo*: Beware!

"All truth, in the long run, is only common sense clarified."
Thomas H. Huxley

Many real estate investment guides on the web and lining your local bookstore's shelves could be rolled into three volumes titled *Abracadabra, Hocus Pocus,* and *Mumbo Jumbo*. These guides are brought to you by wizards with secret spells, magicians who are masters of illusion, and jugglers tossing quick and easy formulas. Some of the most commonly occurring words in titles of real estate books include: "money," "profit," "buy," "flip," "landlord," "guide," "million," "wealth," "fast," "first," "safe" and "rich." Grab a few to combine the header for another trite best seller: *The Millionaire Landlord's Safe Guide to Making Money, Buying, and Flipping Real Estate—Fast.*

And then there are those real estate gurus who package obvious truisms and absurd models under trendy catch phrases of the day, supplemented by publications, promotions, seminars, broadcasts, and consulting gigs. Mainly, more money flows from these promotional empires than from any of the gurus' real estate investments. These gurus claim to reveal wealth-building secrets, but it's mostly common sense clichés wrapped in marketing hype.

If you believe in drive-through, fast-food formulas, then invest in the real estate wizards' rhetoric. Watch your money be magically transported from your wallet to theirs. Keep in mind that *your* money in the guru's wallet is *their* wealth-building secret!

The only genuine secrets in the real estate industry are passed from investor to investor by word of mouth, and only after working with time-tested relationships with financial institutions, buyers, and sellers.

If you're not an insider, though, hard work wins deals over time. Having a clear plan, relentless dedication, fierce determination, and staying on course in the face of adversity will be your path to financial victory. It's back to basics: skipping the easy road to riches, never giving up, having the warrior spirit!

But before entering the realty investment battlefront, ask yourself some tough questions. How serious are you about investing? How much time will you commit? How real are your expectations? How much firepower do you have in your wallet? Are you willing to surmount failures to reach success? Can you honestly muster the dedication, persistence, and hard work to succeed in a cutthroat market? Are you investment-battlefield trained and ready? Or are you sideline struck? Do you have what it takes? Do you understand the real estate you're planning to invest in? If so, you're a combat investor.

In your quest to build your real estate investment war chest, you'll soon realize that success lies beyond gaining square footage. *In the scope of this book, real estate investing is defined as the financial control of the entire premises.* You stand to gain more if you understand the premises, not just the real estate. The property is the real estate as well as anything that can be legally done on premise—everything seen and unseen, including oil and mineral rights, storage space and air rights, and controlling the entire financial battlefield, not just a few fronts.

Why explore real estate investing as warfare? The answer is summed up in two words: territorial control. Who are today's wealthiest landlords? Real estate developers and public realty firms? Yes, this is partially correct. The wealthiest landlords control a collection of premises for industry-related purposes. Dating back to the Industrial Age, these landlords include international energy companies, entertainment moguls, and sports team owners. But the biggest landlords are governments backed by sufficient military power to secure property ownership rights. And in earlier times, landlords controlled kingdoms backed by warrior classes.

As you can see, premises control demands law and order backed by armed forces. Otherwise, private property ownership rights and overall wealth accumulation are limited to those affording their own police force. Ultimately, armed action results from unresolved ownership disputes, such as arrest and eviction. That's territorial gain (or re-gain) using warfare.

Real estate changes hands peacefully with cash or through some form of forced disruption, including eminent domain and lender confiscation. That's territorial gain using real estate investing.

Though military force has been effectively wielded to control real estate since the beginning of time, it's frankly not an acceptable form for territorial gain, unless of course, you're a dictator. Investing strategies, however, do mirror warfare tactics. As a result, the study of successful military principals and blunders and attitudes and behaviors enhance real estate investing strategies.

Also, warfare and real estate investing require dogged persistence for survival. Just as an experienced soldier weathers many battles, a smart investor perseveres through a dizzying array of real estate market cycles. The battle-hardened soldier translates to seasoned investor in the realty wars.

As part of continued survival, warfare and real estate investing skillfully blend intelligence and capital using leading-edge technology for reaching goals. Investing and warfare involve tactical as well as strategic decisions, such as location strategies, resource allocation, and targeting the right premises. Investment decisions and battle aftermaths feature completely unique outcomes, with talented experience separating success from failure.

And even with experience, predicting exact outcomes for either are impossible, but schooling still helps for better results. As with soldiers, combat investors succeed with boots on the ground. Before hitting the financial battlefront, these investment soldiers refine skills with sharpened battle attitudes through real estate investment boot camp.

Real estate investment boot camp is a relatively new training ground. As far back as a century ago, real estate as a dedicated professional discipline was virtually nonexistent. Through the ages, land was bought and sold, then buildings were erected and changed hands. People still made profits from real estate investing.

But historians ignored the art of investing, other than citing architectural and construction milestones. Real estate investing and development focused on empire builders. Did pyramid builders, conquerors, and military leaders author any real estate investment guides? No. Instead, rulers seized the spoils, taking full control of all real estate.

Today's real estate investing offers boot camp training through academia, trade associations, and training organizations. Armed with knowledge, the real estate investor fights on the financial battlefield under better conditions than at any other time in history. Accurate real estate data is no longer limited to a select few. Real estate investing is global, instant, and smart; you need some other competitive advantages to win. Combat investing is one of those advantages.

Combat investing blends fierce discipline, financial engineering, and time-tested investment methods . . . a powerful mix of old and new school knowledge. In the end, successful investing is the precise calibration of today's financial engineering strategies with proven warfare principles for profitable territorial gain.

With combat investing, a consistent, tough, and non-quitting attitude is compulsory for completing boot camp. It's like finishing those extra pushups, when your body says, "No," but your mind pushes beyond. Then, you develop a unique weapons system, a combination of personal operating style, financial capacity, and risk tolerance fueled by this attitude. You're now an investment war machine. You find yourself metaphorically imitating a jet fighter, a tank, a bomber, a helicopter, an aircraft carrier, or perhaps a submarine. You can either attack at close range or "carpet bomb" your deals from a comfortable distance. Different targets with different swag.

That's the beauty of combat investing, the blending of the warrior spirit with real estate investing. No right answer or personal style, just the hunger to succeed. Then, you're done with boot camp.

Shifting your skills and attitude to fight in the investment battlefield is an ongoing process, not just a book, a series of seminars, or a few financial battles. Final victory arises from refining proven behavior patterns with an impersonal, clear-cut intent on filling your realty war chest—your territorial conquest.

Still, many investors fall short of victory by abandoning combat attitudes too quickly when faced with discouraging setbacks. Tackle your fears, focusing only on winning confidence. And remember the occasional failure is the foundation of success. As Thomas Edison said, "I have not failed. I've just found 10,000 ways it won't work."

Over and above combat philosophy, real estate investing has other ties with the military, too many to list. Some obvious and less obvious examples of military origins include: the Internet, the interstate highway system, going green, and digital/satellite imagery. Think of the military the next time you're driving to look at properties using your GPS.

In conclusion, for successful real estate investing, check your attitude first. You must seize the warrior mentality and abandon a scattershot get-rich-quick mindset. Real estate investing is financial warfare—successful investing backed by a fighter's attitude.

Combat Investor is written with this principle in mind. It does not trend hop. Instead, *Combat Investor* tackles real estate investing as a business tapping into a core human instinct—territorialism.

Combat investing is based upon warfare principles with the sole objective of territorial gain for profit. Financial warfare isn't pretty and is often politically incorrect. But it works.

Armed with a combat attitude and a rudimentary understanding of military applications for real estate investing, you have what it takes to be a combat investor. Now take the next step and read on. *Combat Investor: Real Estate Investment Warfare Guide* trains you to become a "land mind" by:

- Unraveling your landgrabbing instincts (Chapter 1).
- Defining real estate investing as your financial war chest (Chapter 2) formulated by assessing various capital risks (Chapter 3), measuring your thirst for battle (Chapter 4), and identifying your individual combat investor "style" (Chapter 5).
- Targeting battlefields based upon locations and property types (Chapter 6).
- Training you to fight in current and future investment battlefronts (Chapter 7) according to proven military tactics for striking profitable targets (Chapter 8).

If you're starting to see real estate investing through the eyes of a warrior, then join the ranks of combat investors. Crack those knuckles and get going!

Let's start by tapping into your landgrabbing instincts . . .

CHAPTER 1

LANDGRABBING: PRIMAL INSTINCT

"He that has lands has quarrels."
English saying

Landgrabbing is a primal instinct. As a property owner, you're either content in financially protecting your assets or looking to expand your holdings. You're either prey or predator. You're always on call . . . willing, able, and ready for financial war!

Landgrabbing warfare is latent or active. History cycles through periods of tension, threats, combat, and pauses for peace. These are all different states of landgrabbing. If not in the state of combat, an investor is anxious—constantly on the verge of an offensive or defensive move of capturing or protecting territory.

War is explosive but not random. Every fire requires a spark. Unleashed aggression is the fuse; it's dormant if tempered with tolerance. The emotions fueling aggression—greed, power, jealousy, and anger—are the same that ignite real estate investment decisions, only in a commercial context. The warrior and the investor share objectives—the landgrab. To stage a victorious offensive, both require the following:

- **Deliberate Action**
  Control and improvement of land entails a premeditated plan of action.

- **Capital**
  Building weapons, assembling armies, and purchasing property all involve money—either up front or borrowed in the form of war bonds or mortgages.

- **Talent/Technology**
  Gaining the winning advantage requires brainpower and the tool that converts brainpower into action—technology.

- **Risk/Reward**
  Risk and reward are inherent in any venture. A warrior risks life; an investor risks cash. Winning big means risking big.

- **Negotiation**
  A conqueror doesn't have to be noble to partake in negotiations—the conqueror sees it as a means to an end. Invaders force resolution, in conquest as well as in acquisition. A negotiation may be lost, but then the warrior and combat investor will fight another day. Does it have to be this way, or can peace be found? The landgrab is incomplete without filling your war chest.

Even if your pockets are sagging under the weight of dirt (land) and profits, you still have the tendency to reach out and expand your holdings. This territorialism is the essence of filling your war chest. Territorialism can be good or bad, constructive (combat investor's viewpoint) or destructive.

CONSTRUCTIVE LANDGRABS

Some forms of territorial expansion are constructive and seem purely benign, though the combat investor should still view them in the context of a rough-and-tumble market. Some sample positive spins on landgrabbing along with the combat investor's blunt interpretations are as follows:

- **Homeownership**

  - *Constructive.* We all know that homeownership remains the American Dream. The home is a castle; the owner is a king. After all, who hasn't sat through a dinner party listening to someone bragging about great deals made when buying or selling a home?

  - *Combat investor.* The American Dream requires ammunition (cash) and the willingness to strike (aggression) to get the property you want. This is your first step in the real estate investing game.

- **Shopping Center Development**

  - *Constructive.* This provides a better shopping experience. Visit some of the new, trendy retailers in a safe and convenient setting with ample parking.

Everyone wants a fun and exciting place to meet, dine, and shop.

- o *Combat investor.* The state-of-the-art shopping center competes with other entertainment and shopping venues for consumer dollars in the area. Generate higher revenues by offering new (or upgraded) facilities. Weaker retailers and older centers will lose market share, but newer centers attract more tenants and shoppers. Simple math.

- **High-Rise Apartment Complex**

  - o *Constructive.* The lack of affordable single-family housing fuels demand for a new multifamily development. The goal is to provide a multitude of pricing options for those choosing a carefree rental lifestyle.

  - o *Combat investor.* Multifamily properties are the most desirable investments, offering inflation protection with annual rental increases. Ongoing housing shortages promise growing demand for this product type.

- **New Government Office**

  - o *Constructive.* A public enterprise that serves taxpayers with improved facilities.

  - o *Combat investor.* This is a territorial expansion of a governmental body. A new building means more tax dollars appropriated to the agency, its employees, the surrounding area, and local politicians. Agencies must compete with other public and private organizations for survival.

- **House of Worship Expansion**

  - *Constructive.* Upgraded house of prayer offers the best worship facilities for the congregation.

  - *Combat investor.* Modernized facilities assure survival of the religious organization by updating property. Churches compete with other nonprofit groups for charitable funds. Inspired worshippers are likely to donate more.

Be it profit or nonprofit, the intentions are the same: keep the paying, space-using consumer satisfied while maintaining the competitive territorial growth essential to survival. Such territorial plays become "win-win" scenarios for the giver and user of the premises.

DESTRUCTIVE LANDGRABS

Here's where landgrabbing gets ugly. When territorial gain cannot be voluntarily completed with mutually beneficial transfer of property, landgrabbing is destructive and confrontations erupt. Destructive landgrabs create collateral damage and acts of realty recklessness—deforestation, strip mining, flash dumping, and unchecked urban sprawl.

Negatively-motivated territorial instincts are always at work. Every day somewhere on the planet, dissatisfied people fight over borders, mineral and water rights, arable land, port access, and other real property issues. On the local level, that warfare is seen in property line quarrels, tenant/landlord clashes, and lender/borrower disputes. If disagreements remain unsolved, war is the ultimate solution.

War, or some type of military action, forcibly resolves disputes. Be it a police arrest or private land confiscation by eminent domain, governmental bodies use sanctioned force. Losers suffer financial loss, imprisonment, or worse. Victors grab the real estate. With a series of such continued successes, victors become empire builders—realty investors by default.

EMPIRE BUILDERS

"All empires have been cemented in blood."
Edmund Burke

Talent drives technology and civilization but also destroys it. Pre-industrial era kings, queens, religious leaders, and warlords wielded the newest weapons and military power to decimate the conquered. Though information technology has rewritten today's rules of engagement; the process of future change is far from stagnant. History repeatedly teaches us how the past shapes future empires. Creative problem solving and applied technologies distinguished victorious combat investors with their empires during each of the following eras:

- **Colonization**
  The bloodiest incarnation of real estate investing involves colonization. Combat investors gain territorial control by grabbing the resources of a weaker society. Spawning national identity, monarchs recruit large armies from mostly agrarian populations. Then, they cultivate battlefield

innovation to gain advantage over potential colonies. Territorial growth occurs through armed conflict.

- **Industrialization**
  Improved manufacturing techniques draw workers from fields to higher paying jobs in factories. The combat investor evolves into an industrialist by grabbing resources for manufacturing and controlling distribution. Combat investing becomes a land monopoly play with smokestacks running at full steam.

- **Consumerization**
  To the mall y'all! Realizing that sharing wealth begets more wealth, combat investors expand into consumption-oriented real estate. Larger homes with spacious backyards, enclosed shopping malls, entertainment districts, theme parks, resorts, spas, health clubs, golf courses, and other realty amenities sprawl across the landscape at unprecedented levels. Everyone wants the American Dream. Bigger is better. Combat investor to the rescue!

- **Optimization**
  Trim the fat and find a lifestyle balance. The combat investor shifts gears. It is not the mere size but the quality of space that is most significant. Smaller space is more desirable if the investment is within an infill location serving a more densely populated area. The combat investor's portfolio is aimed at smart real estate—land and buildings with brains. Zero is the hero! Zero footprint. Zero emission.

Whether technology and other changes will lead to more growth or destruction in the coming empires is a delicate question for society and real estate combat investing. In reality, it's a mixture of both, with the hope of a favorable outcome. And any part of such discussions brings in erasing falsehoods and misconceptions about empires.

CRUSHING THE MYTHS

"War is the admission of defeat in the face of conflicting interests."

German Greer

How have empires been built throughout the eras?

Let's explore what empires are all about, eliminating any myths. According to Webster's Revised Unabridged Dictionary (1913 Edition), an *empire* is "a political unit having an extensive territory or comprising a number of territories or nations and ruled by a single supreme authority." That's real estate investment in a nutshell.

The world's greatest empire builders—Egyptians, Chinese, Greeks, Romans, Byzantines, British, French, and Americans—all developed social and physical infrastructures backed by strong military as well as economic power. These empires vastly expanded territorial holdings through successful warfare-and-plunder campaigns that created great transfers of wealth, fueling further growth and expansion.

Are you wondering about wars fought for noble reasons unrelated to landgrabbing like religion or patriotism? Don't be naive. Not all empire builders labeled themselves as landgrabbers, but all of them ultimately practiced territorial expansion.

All victors do landgrabs. They win, they stay, and they set up shop. Sometimes these uninvited guests share spoils with the cooperative conquered. Even after withdrawing troops, victorious conquerors maintain some form of ongoing, indirect control over the conquered lands. But are these conquerors good guys or bad guys? Fame or shame?

HALL OF FAME OR SHAME?

"Every designer's dirty little secret is that they copy other designers' work. They see work they like, and they imitate it. Rather cheekily, they call this inspiration."

Aaron Russell

Deserving fame or shame (defined diametrically by the victorious and the conquered), the greatest rulers in modern history have permanently transformed the face of real estate investing. Some of the most skilled and prolific combat investors—energy barons, merchandisers, religious leaders, and of course, governments—never perceived real estate as an investment in and of itself but as a tool fueling ambition.

A combat investor need not be a real estate professional per se—in fact, most are entrepreneurs using real estate as the underlying asset. Upon reaching success, they become combat investors by default, using cash flow to spawn territorial expansion, and fiercely packing the war chests. Depending on behavior, investors could be good or bad guys.

Combat investors are not necessarily the inventors or creators of unique products or services. Rather, they convert creative concepts into successful realty-based actions. These opportunists take advantage of territorial expansion through oil fields, dealerships, franchises, religious buildings, or any other real estate type that yields territorial advantage for the cultivation of their activities.

They're not necessarily the first to get the product on the market, but the first ones to capitalize on it. Judging actions individually, these combat investors could be good or bad guys.

The most active, low-profile, and large-scale combat investors are the financial institutions. Such institutions usually invest indirectly, by lending capital to entrepreneurs and corporations. In particular, insurance companies remain active as longer-term real estate investments are well-matched to insurers' cash flow timelines. In boom times, insurers are lenders for real estate; during busts, they become unwilling owners. These conservative institutions maintain low profiles and are difficult to identify as combat investors. Banks, too, are key investors, but such sources of funds are shorter-term, limited to acquisition and development capital.

How are these different types of combat investors trained to be successful? For starters, real estate investing is a broadly-defined field. Originally classified as part of land use economics, real estate investing wasn't recognized as a formal discipline prior to World War II, and therefore, published literature is scant from that era.

Historically speaking, coverage of real estate investing was limited to local publications' stories about successful individuals in the markets. Some national real estate investment formats gained headline notoriety. The gold bonds of the 1920s were probably the first organized effort to promote public investing in realty securities, but these investment vehicles succumbed to the Crash of 1929.

The pre-World War II combat investor legends were trained as American industrialists. Combined with both positive and negative elements, these industrialists built much of the country we know today. Early profit and nonprofit industrialists enjoyed unfettered territorial expansion until the government stepped in to curb it. Examples of these legendary combat investors include: John Rockefeller, who assembled an oil superpower to fuel the industrialization; Henry Ford, who spawned and spread assembly line production; and lesser known, General Robert E. Wood, who transformed Sears Roebuck from a catalog house to a retailing pioneer that reached into every corner of the burgeoning consumer age.

- **John D. Rockefeller**
  "If you want to succeed, you should strike out on new paths, rather than travel the worn paths of accepted success."

The quintessential capitalist and billionaire, Rockefeller channeled his uncanny combat investor abilities into assembling land for oil production, amassing what is the world's largest energy processing empire. The world's largest energy corporations trace their origins to the Rockefeller family. Their petroleum powers nearly every type of transportation form used today including air, land, and sea equipment. Availability of fuel made transportation much faster and more expansive, opening up even outer space options. It made space/time usage of square feet infinitely more efficient.

- **Henry Ford**
  "Nothing is particularly hard if you divide it into small jobs."

Literally fueled by Rockefeller's oil, Henry Ford transformed the real estate investment landscape again by bringing personal freedom of movement to the masses. The mass production of the automobile expanded real estate investing to encompass any road-accessible location. Ford's assembly line also expanded the concept of territorial gain from a cottage industry to a manufacturing process, diversifying into dealerships, which paved the way for future generations of combat investors. The amount of square footage conquered by the automotive industry certainly ranks as one of the greatest land plays in history.

- **General Robert E. Wood**
"Business is like war in one respect. If its grand strategy is correct, any number of tactical errors can be made and yet the enterprise proves successful."

Though he is probably the least known member of the Combat Investor Hall of Fame, General Robert E. Wood's retail territorial gains on a national and international scale are unparalleled. After military service in Panama early in the twentieth century, Wood transformed Sears Roebuck from a mail-order catalog plant into a powerhouse retailer with stores built at nearly every key commercial intersection in the nation. Wood's most important real estate contribution is the transformation of site selection into a dedicated discipline with market statistics analysis. His methodology became standard for any knowledgeable real estate investor. Since then, many retailers emulated and perfected the strategic planning techniques he used to build his retail empire (for example, Walmart and Target).

Real estate investing evolved into a more formal discipline during the latter half of the twentieth century. Legendary real estate

developers Bill Zeckendorf, Trammell Crow, Marshall Bennett,
the Bohannons, the Trumps, and Bucksbaums as well as others
elevated real estate development into an organized full-time
profession. Large-scale combat investing was no longer limited to
corporate America or industrial entrepreneurs, as developers with
land assemblage and property management expertise started to
proliferate nationally.

Real estate investing as a discipline grew more bold and daring.
Visionaries started constructing "spec" commercial projects
in new outlying suburban areas. Open fields transformed into
densely-developed suburban communities, greatly facilitating
land assemblage. Advanced construction and design technologies
and personal transportation spurred large-scale affordable
development. Industrial parks, intermodal distribution, suburban
tract development, strip shopping centers, malls, and bedroom
communities radicalized the concept of territorial gain with new
landscapes centered upon the automobile. Those contributing
most to these new real estate realities include: President Dwight
Eisenhower, whose interstate highway system provided the
infrastructure base for a new land-use policy; New York developer
William Zeckendorf, the master of the complicated deal including
operating leases, land-sale leasebacks, and junior and senior debt
positions; residential developer William Levitt, whose Levittown
showed how housing could be made affordable for the average
family; and hamburger titan Ray Kroc, whose McDonald's
franchising transformed retailing and real estate.

Now, real estate investment is no longer a new frontier or the "wild,
wild West." Even so, we have much more to learn as significant
changes are underway with militarily trained realty professionals
leading the charge.

TODAY'S COMBAT INVESTORS

This country extols a landscape of successful real estate entrepreneurs and investors. Many served in the armed forces, often attributing their realty successes to military training as a career framework. Real estate superstars include:

- **Ron Terwilliger**, head of Trammell Crow Residential, one of the nation's largest multifamily developers. Terwilliger, a graduate of the United States Naval Academy, led the firm into national prominence within this property sector for more than twenty years. Terwilliger actively promotes and supports national policies for affordable housing.

- **Roger Staubach,** Hall of Fame former professional football star quarterback of the Dallas Cowboys. Now a renowned commercial real estate broker and property owner, he successfully created a national brokerage firm that recently merged with an international realty firm. Staubach is also a United States Naval Academy graduate. He is an excellent example of how the competitive sports spirit, combined with military training, provides for continued success in the real estate investment arena.

- **Donald Trump**, owner/founder, The Trump Organization, developer/author and military school graduate. Trump understands how to effectively use luxury as product branding for his premises, covering all forms of the media.

Countless other real estate investors with or without military training will inevitably surface into prominence, creating war chests of all shapes and sizes. Now, let's discuss how you will build your own war chest.

CHAPTER 2

THINKING INSIDE THE BOX:
FINDING YOUR WAR CHEST

"Property is intended to serve life, and no matter how much we surround it with rights and respect, it has no personal being. It is part of the earth man walks on. It is not man."

Martin Luther King Jr.

To invest in real estate means to understand how it is used. Real estate is the common denominator of all social and commercial activities. Everyone demands a place to live, work, and play—whether it's a cave, skyscraper, home, shopping mall, or factory. The roof over your head is a more imperative investment than stocks, bonds, or even your smartphone! Since every human activity requires controlling and occupying space (territorialism), the combat investor's mantra is, "Premises, premises, premises."

Why premises and not real property or real estate holdings? Real property definitions are limited to immovable assets fixed in place within an exact location—the traditional view of real estate. In contrast, premises expand beyond just real property. The Latin root "pre" means "placed before," emphasizing the primacy of territorial pursuits. The definition of premises—the buildings and land that a business or organization uses—accurately describes the scope of combat investing. Since the term applies to both the singular and plural forms, it reflects the dynamism of real estate, with varied uses by businesses, individuals, and organizations. It embodies the three-dimensionality of real estate in form and function, a dimensionality best illustrated inside the box or cube. In military terms, a war chest.

To prepare for the investing battlefield, start thinking about real estate in a multi-dimensional framework—a series of war chests. Most how-to books treat real estate cash flow as a two-dimensional exercise, citing monthly rent, square feet rates, room revenue per night, dollars per parking space, etc. College textbooks present the subject in a more detailed, three-dimensional format—as a multi-disciplinary concept blending business, engineering, architecture, construction, finance, and urban planning. Let's take another look at real estate as a space/time/cost unit.

THE SHRINKING SQUARE FOOT

"Design is not the narrow application of formal skills; it is a way of thinking."

Chris Pullman

The shrinking square foot is the new reality in the marketplace. As the global population increases, property usage is more dense and costly, a similar comparison in modern warfare often restricted to smaller, scattered battlefronts fought block to block, not in an open battlefield.

But is the square foot shrinking, or are property owners inefficiently using their premises? Rather than shrinking, this measurement unit is morphing by expanding up, out, and taking different shapes.

- **Moving up**
  Recovering excess vertical space, as in stacking more boxes in a warehouse or stacking higher levels in built-in shelving.

- **Moving out**
  Destruction or abandonment, as in demolishing a decrepit building or vacating a toxic site.

- **Morphing**
  Finding a more efficient and profitable use for premises, as in transforming an obsolete office building into a senior living facility.

Real estate includes dumb space and smart space. The dumb space is relegated to a lower use or even destruction. An outdated industrial manufacturing plant, for example, is converted into self-storage space. If the savvy investor is unable to utilize dumb space, it will soon be invited to the wrecker's ball. Operating mediocre, inefficient space is simply too expensive.

Smart space, on the other hand, conquers the competition with cost-effectiveness. Informed investors work with designers and space planners to maximize usage, eyeing cash flow where others see vacant space and quickly fill the value gap.

To understand real estate as a commodity, delve beyond square-foot and per-room calculations. In keeping with emerging technology and population trends, real estate is truly multi-spatial, so the savvy investor:

- defines the real estate usages within a given space/time dimension
- identifies various potential real estate users
- accommodates those usages within a cost-effective and profitable fee structure

What's the best way to comprehend real estate profitability and usage in any form or shape? Let's talk about the war chest, the cash flow space which applies to not only financial modeling but also to defining the investment battlefield itself. The combat investor visualizes a real estate investing opportunity as a war chest, a three-dimensional measurement of space, time, and money on the premises and an opportunity encumbering the investor's financial objectives. The war chest is the booty, the investor's reward.

For each conquered premises, an investor sets into motion a war chest that synthesizes space, time, and usage fees into cash flow.

1. A landlord charges a usage fee to a tenant for a space that's being occupied for a specified amount of time (a space/time unit).
2. In turn, the time meter begins ticking for the duration of this unit's usage at the usage rate (for example, ticket price, monthly bill, hourly rental, lump sum payment, etc.).
3. A war chest is generated for that space/time unit and spinning at the speed of the usage rate to create cash flow in the form of profit to the landlord or cost to the user.

THE SPACE/TIME UNIT

"In the air, on land, and sea."
Marines' Hymn

Real estate usage is like gelatin. It takes on the form of the mold a user requires to create a home, business, office, entertainment venue, or warehouse environment. This form is quantified in the space/time unit that becomes the content of the war chest.

Combat investors own and control the premises; tenants are users. The owner pays operating costs; the tenant pays usage costs. Excess financial gains or losses flow to the controlling party, which pays operating costs even when the premises are vacant. If the owner also occupies the space, absorbing an opportunity cost, potential profits are eliminated. Usage remains free as long as the owner of the premises is not charging any fees. Once fees are charged, the premises trigger a real estate investment and the war chest holds some valuable contents.

Real estate usage fees apply to all premises, whether profit or nonprofit. A church visit requires a donation (hopefully). An office space requires rent payments. Home-dwelling requires tax payments. If space is being occupied, *someone* is paying for it. For the war chest, nearly any activity that occupies space is construed as a space/time unit. Some examples are:

- movie theater seat
- cemetery plot
- baseball game bench
- hospital room
- office space
- shopping mall kiosk

- self-storage locker
- church pew
- convention hall
- garage space
- barstool
- swimming pool
- cafe table

In real estate terms, space is a three-dimensional fixed location or resource on, above, or below the earth's surface tied to land, air, water, and mineral rights. Investors should keep in mind all of these components of space that contain additional productivity opportunities above and beyond the surface. As technology progresses, outer space will be part of this definition. To paraphrase the marine hymn that embodies the combat investor philosophy, in the air, on land, and sea—space/time units are stashed in everyone's war chest. The premises usage encompasses all aspects including at grade, above grade, below grade, submerged, and airspace.

- **Above grade**
  Otherwise known as "vertical," this is the most traditional form of real estate improvements, which includes all property developments on the planet's surface.

- **At grade**
  Encompasses all unimproved land including deserts, prairies, farmland, mountain ranges, and any other land not covered by water.

- **Below grade**
  Any improved or unimproved areas below grade and not covered by water. Includes underground structures, minerals, thermal heat, oil, and natural gas.

- **Submerged**

  Any land covered by water. Mountain ranges beneath oceans are constantly expanding with volcanic activity, creating new land masses and rising tides created by global warming.

- **Airspace**

  Space above the improvement belongs to the land in the form of air rights. Air rights are gaining significance as cleaner air and technological advances open this frontier to new uses. Imagine in the not-too-distant future, 3-D holograms projecting ads into the sky; a new definition of airspace will develop. Future generations will deploy outer space beyond the earth's atmosphere. The sky is *not* the limit for the combat investor, just another battlefront to conquer.

TIME METERING

Upon defining the space/time units inside your war chest, a time meter ticks, calibrating the time duration with money. The space is used over a defined timeframe, be it for a brief moment, hours, days, months, years, or even in perpetuity. In combat investment terms, time metering defines how long to plan for staying on the battlefield and whether to expand or contract the war chest. In this context, time is categorized into four formats: function, event, contractual, and perpetual. Time increments vary based on the investment type.

- **Function Time**

  Function time measurements are limited to a generally stationary activity. Functions span less than a minute to days—however long it takes to complete a function(s). Examples include:

- travel: the duration of journey
- vending machine purchase: less than one minute
- arcade game: one to five minutes
- gas station fill-up: five to ten minutes
- restaurant visit: ten minutes to three hours
- medical treatment/hospital stay: one hour or more

- **Event Time**

  When individuals gather in an exact location to share a specific experience, events occur where time is calculable. The investments are public, private, or nonprofit. If public events are not taxpayer-funded, admission fees are assessed. The space/time unit may be seating, standing room, or even lying down, as during a casual outdoor concert. Other examples include:

  - football/soccer/hockey/basketball/baseball game: three to five hours using quarter units with intermission
  - concert: three to five hours
  - protest/rally: one to five hours
  - worship service: one to three hours

- **Contractual Time**

  The agreed upon term is limited by a signed contract, which specifies the rate and any other pricing adjustments during the timeframe.

- standard school day: five to eight hours
- standard office work day: eight to 12 hours
- lodging complex: room night
- national park: daily and annual pass
- apartment: monthly rent with an annual contract
- storage facilities: daily, weekly, monthly, quarterly or longer
- typical commercial lease: five to 25 years
- prison sentence: time period delegated by court order

- **Perpetual Time**

  In this open-ended paradigm, the duration is assumed to be in perpetuity. Costs are paid upfront and maintenance fees applied in the form of taxes and annual fees.

  - cemetery plot
  - forest preserve: lifetime license to use as a taxpayer

These time meter formats encompass space/time activities not being interchangeable. For instance, you wouldn't request a perpetual lease on an apartment, or security officials would surely greet you for trying to stay in the ballpark for extra hours after the game.

The realty time masters are timesharing companies that have subdivided their clocks into much more profitable war chests. To the combat investor, the war chest is carefully metered; otherwise, time is stolen. A cash flow burglar lurks in every vacant basement storage space, in every stash of unused furniture, and in many other unsuspected nooks and crannies. In such cases it's not to say that every portion of your premises should be usable. However, you should be aware of a money-leaking money war chest—paying for space not being used.

THE WAR CHEST

"Riches do not consist in the possession of treasures, but in the use made of them."

—Napoleon Bonaparte

The combat investor's measure of territorial gain expands beyond controlling the premises by adding profitability to the equation. The upper hand hovering over the war chest represents the investor *offering* cubic space to the user (the hand below), who is *receiving* the space over a predefined time period for a premises usage fee. The swirling golden arrow around the war chest indicates changing market conditions, competition, new technologies, and other forces propelling or slowing down the war chest's motion, either as profits or losses.

For the combat investor, knowing battlefield profitability is the difference between victory and defeat. The war chest exposes the battlefield, accounting for various possible premises' usage scenarios by private, public, and nonprofit sectors. These sectors control their own premises as a matter of financial survival, adjusting to varying degrees of profitability, be it for maximum profit or for operational efficiency. The single and multiple war chests explain usage from a different perspective:

- **The Single War Chest**

  The single war chest is limited to only one type of space/ time use on the investor's premises. For the combat investor, this chest is a one-dimensional attack plan without alternative scenarios in the case of failure. It's either hit or miss.

  The simplest example of a single war chest is a metered parking space. A footprint (space) is provided for temporary parking (usage) and equipped with a meter (usage fee), which expires (time) at a time depending on the amount of coins paid. At the end of the day, the owner empties out the meter (cash flow). The space requires a reasonable time limit, as other drivers await their turns for the spot. If parking spaces are the only investment alternative for the premises, you're a one-trick pony.

  Looking to expand beyond the parking meter and, perhaps add a billboard on-site or an ATM machine? If so, you now have multiple war chests for gaining more ground in the investment battlefield.

- **The Multiple War Chests**

Finding many war chests for on the premises is good. Most premises feature multiple war chests, especially those operated by creative investors.

A movie theater is a good example. Patrons buy a ticket (usage fee), sit in a theater chair (space), watch a movie for two hours (time), and enjoy an entertainment venue (usage), which generates various war chests for the ownership (real estate investment). Of course, the most obvious war chest is a theater seat generating revenue for about a two-hour duration. Other war chests on the theater premises include an arcade area, party rental room, soda vending machine, and the snack bar. Even the washroom stalls have advertising revenue, so no part of the premises is sacred!

In the field of combat investing, every financial decision centers upon enriching the war chests. Just as the military commander covers land, sea, and air operations, the combat investor tackles time, space, and profitable usage. Successful projects generate several dimensions of value, responsibly using labor and capital to conquer and optimize the premises. What are the premises you've made or kept?

CHAPTER 3

PREMISES MADE, PREMISES KEPT: REALTY CAPITAL AT WORK

"The best investment on earth is earth."
Louis Glickman

Capital organically gravitates toward real estate, the world's investing cornerstone—over two-thirds of America's wealth is invested in real estate.

Who's doing the investing? Everybody! Individuals, syndicators, high net worth investors, hedge funds, pension funds, foreign investors, real estate investment trusts, banks, insurance companies, and Wall Street securitized funds. When preparing battle plans, combat investors measure their financial strength (capital) and effectiveness of their forces (yield) for striking a target (the premises).

The ultimate goal of any combat investor is to maximize profit while minimizing risk—conquering the most territory with minimal financial casualties. How? By building richer war chests using capital budgeting weaponry for "slicing and dicing" risk.

THE SHARP KNIFE CALLED RISK

The combat investor's most important survival weapon is the risk knife. This knife is handled with great care as it can save or hurt you, depending on your weapons training and battlefield conditions. With knife in hand, you're ready to defend or attack with clear-cut decisions. How should you handle this delicate, yet critically important weapon?

When chasing your passion, whether for financial gain, emotional fulfillment, or thrills, you have to ask yourself what price you are willing to pay to succeed, to win it all. How sharp is your risk knife? Let's develop a clear understanding of the trade-off between the return you are expecting from an investment—the war chest prize—and the degree of risk assumed to earn that return.

Realty investment risks include many variables that are controllable and non-controllable. Effective risk management focuses on understanding non-controllable risks and proactively managing controllable risks.

Controllable risk is how you handle the knife to create and protect your war chest, keeping it sharp and always practicing your skills. Controllable risk factors are inherent to the investor and property, such as management expertise, operating capital, funding leverage, and property condition. The most common examples include:

- property risks based upon age, overall physical and structural condition, and environmental and functional obsolescence
- premises risk such as current zoning, environmental remediation, ingress and egress, tenant rent roll, and credit profiles
- cash flow performance risks in the form of cash flow, tenant roster, income collection, and performance
- leverage risk relating to amount of debt, interest rates, debt coverage ratios, fixed or floating rate exposure, type of loan and term, prepayment provisions, and assumability
- sponsorship risks linked to ownership cash liquidity, management expertise, market knowledge, and investment savvy

Non-controllable risk is how the knife is actually used in combat. How you use your weapon in real life, not practice training. How you attack and protect war chests in the thick of battle. Non-controllable real estate risks are outside the scope of the investment as shown in the following examples:

- overall local and national economic conditions based upon unemployment, interest rates, job growth, and recessionary and inflationary pressures
- locational factors relating to market dynamics—mainly supply and demand balance that you do not control
- governance, including the political conditions, budgetary constraints, and other factors effecting policies relating to zoning, property taxation, and employee taxes

The *risk/return tradeoff* (what's been called the ability-to-sleep-at-night test) is the balance between the desire for the lowest risk and the highest profit—how to keep a lock on your war chest without losing or breaking the keys. While these principles are elementary to any investment, they're worth repeating as many people frequently overlook the big picture of financial return.

- **Return *of* Capital**
  You want to get back *at least* what you've invested—hopefully more. In warfare, the equivalent to return of capital is coming back alive. The *minimum* goal of any investment—keeping the war chest.

- **Return *on* Capital**
  Once proven that your money is fully repayable, prepare to capture profits (or yield, gain, equity return, positive cash flow, and staying/being "in the black"). In the military, it's called gaining ground, the goal of any investment—filling the war chest.

- **Law of Principal and Interest**
  Investors want to fund projects with the expectation of receiving their original investment back (return *of*

capital) along with a profit (return *on* capital or interest (yield)—keeping *and* filling the war chest.

In the final analysis, the risk knife makes the cleanest cuts with minimum harm done to the investor handling it. The delicate balance relates to return *of* and *on* capital.

Once you've successfully attained return of capital, you will naturally hunger for more. The war chest is somewhat empty. Greed, after all, fuels war and territorial expansion. But how greedy should you be? How much should you share?

Since greed is self-governing, each investor devises personal benchmarks. It's knowing where you are in the field of combat. When yield (the polite term for financial greed) is the only *monetary* reason for investing, and if content with a given yield(s), then consider *yourself* successful. The war chest is full.

The risk is translated to yield in real estate investing as illustrated in the RateStack.

RATESTACK—IS YOUR WAR CHEST TOO HEAVY?

"Based on my own personal experience—both as an investor in recent years and an expert witness in years past—rarely do more than three or four variables really count. Everything else is noise."

Marty Whitman

The RateStack is the combat investor's fulcrum for weighing the risk loan of the war chest. For the combat investor, the RateStack weighs each investment for risk load balanced by leverage (the ability to use other people's money to amplify profits). In addition, the RateStack is shaped like a pyramid for placing your war chest on top to also find the correct risk/reward equilibrium and tipping points—the right balance.

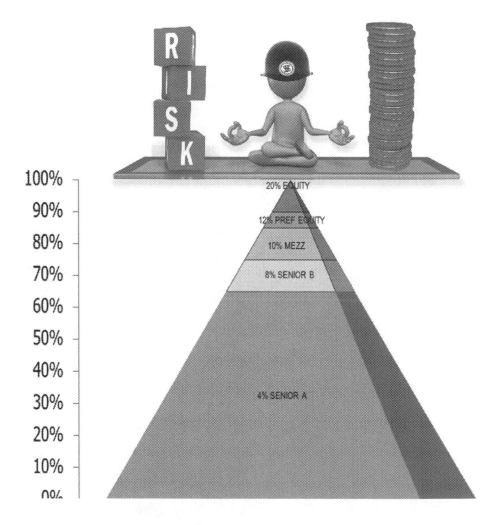

The RateStack measures project investment capital in order of risk including: pure debt (a senior mortgage); hybrid debt, classified as any type of extraordinary financing nestled between the mortgage and cash down payment; and of course, the investor equity—cash in the deal. The stack contains the most risk at the top of the pyramid, sliding downward to the position with the least risk. Higher positions in the stack expect higher returns. Lenders and equity stakeholders are extremely sensitive to their position in the stack. The bottom green zone represents safe yields; the top red zone indicates risky yields.

As with an actual pyramid, the highest amount of wear and tear is at the tip where the war chest sits balanced, while the base has the most safety and stability. In this example, the bottom of the pyramid shows the safest return as a mortgage yielding 4%, while the equity yield is as high as 20% (or more).

Leverage is how much help you'll have in carrying your war chest. No leverage means you carry the war chest yourself. Full leverage means others are bearing the load. The leverage ratios help to determine how to properly balance the war chest load. Too much leverage could mean the war chest will fall and bust very easily if conditions change. Leverage availability is displayed as a backdrop within yield range, spanning from zero (all-cash) to 100% (full) leverage. Equity yields represent the pyramid tip within a leverage range of 90-100%, while less risky yields (approximately 65% or less) stand a better chance of principal recovery in the event of financial failure.

Using the RateStack, let's expand on the discussion of real estate yields and leverage ranges within historical norms—acceptable weight and balance ratios for your war chest.

YIELD

Throughout most of this decade, green yields have ranged between 5% and 7%, while red yields top 15% overall returns (the traditional high-water mark for conservative institutional investments). This is known as Core and Core Plus real estate. Core identifies the finest quality properties in the marketplace; Core Plus adds slightly more risk including tenant rollover, lower-grade credit profiles, and secondary location.

What about investment returns that are substantially over 15%? After all, investors are known for doubling returns within a few years. Even an infinite return is possible with no money down! Targeting such high returns means seeking development projects and carrying very heavy war chests with lots of help. Investors use opportunity funds for chasing such deals including new construction, redevelopment, and substantial repositioning of properties.

The optimal deployment of capital with acceptable yields is the backbone of all investment decisions. When done right, premises made are premises kept inside your war chest.

Now that you understand how to handle a risk knife and a balanced war chest, it's time for boot camp. Boot camp tests your ability to lift and carry the war chest.

CHAPTER 4

BOOT CAMP: EXPLORING YOUR AMBITION, RISK TOLERANCE, AND TALENT

HIPPIE PEACE OR NASTY WAR?

"A great many people enjoy a war provided it's not in their neighborhood and not too bad."

Bertrand Russell

Before stepping foot into boot camp, do you prefer butter over guns? Do you believe that victory is easy to share? Do you fully trust human nature? If so, you're not alone, as we all strive for peace and harmony.

The hippies of the 1960s hungered for an ideal life, while enjoying a strong economy. Disgusted with the war and military spending, hippies gravitated toward goodness instead of evil. All well-intentioned. No death or destruction from warfare. No guns, just butter. This same generation witnessed some of the best real estate investment market conditions ever. Easy credit, full employment, and limited governmental regulations drove economic prosperity. The real estate hippie's peacetime meant no-money-down easy deals and nearly boundless profit opportunities without significant restrictions.

Unfortunately, the hippie peacetime was an illusion. Good intentions collided with reality. Boundless real estate development resulted in urban sprawl. A carefree regulatory environment was replaced by burdensome rules and regulations. Too much of a good thing isn't. Everyone wanted in, but not enough wealth to share. Not enough landgrab booty.

For the combat investor, this is reality—the constant flux between conflict and peace (yin and yang). This eternal conflict elicits the best and worst in human nature, generating investing in its purest form. Once the delicate balance is disturbed, pent-up aggression is let loose, and combat investing begins. Does it really have to be so offensive, so messy? In a word, "Yes."

"ALWAYS BE CLOSING"

"Always Be Closing" is the relentless marching pace set for real estate brokers in the movie *Glengarry Glen Ross* (1992). Perform or get fired. No lunch breaks or playing cards with the buddies. No friendly water cooler chatter about the kids. Everyone's out for themselves and their commissions. The *Glengarry Glen Ross* system rewards performance. It's driven by clear, concise, quantifiable goals and reinforced by fear. When failure is punished and greed rewarded, only the fittest survive. "Always Be Closing" exemplifies the proactive, *offensive* (in the military and civilian sense) attitude of the combat investor in the work environment.

Real estate investment reality shocks innocent Bambi. A sweet, kind, cute, and gentle character starts out loved by all and threatened by none. At first, no predators are in sight. The forest is a beautiful place, and life is simple and easy. Until . . . fire! The forest animals aren't ready or equipped to fight the flames. They scatter for the hills or perish.

When the crisis came, more forest dwellers could have been saved if better forewarned or prepared. To promote a fairy tale, Bambi's work environment was to create a false sense of security.

Crises are inevitable in real estate investing—sloppy deals, misrepresentations, incompetence, unreliable forecasts, lawsuits, and cost overruns. Bambi showed the *defensive* response of the ill-prepared. Reaction, not an action. Flight, instead of fight.

The "Always Be Closing" strategy is blunt and direct; Bambi's is passive and reactive. Combat investors choose the former, and smart investors customize their approach as follows: diplomatic and graceful or harshly confrontational; conciliatory or argumentative; and consensus-building team play or lone wolf attacks.

Boot camp is tough and promotes the "Always Be Closing" attitude. You have to be honest with yourself and understand your talents and limitations. You need to look at yourself in the mirror.

"We have met the enemy, and he is us."
Walt Kelly

SUICIDE BOMBERS CRASH INTO MIRRORS

All real estate investors have the potential to become financial suicide bombers and blow up their own holdings when armed with unsuitable advice or faulty follow-through. If practicing safe and savvy investing, however, any loose bombs are defused. Combat investor or combat victim—the choice is yours. Build or drop the war chest.

Talent is essential ammunition for a combat investor. It's the labor in Adam Smith's "land, labor and capital" equation. Talent requires constant reloading through boot camps. Talent is of the highest caliber and embodies the latest technologies to ensure precision, accuracy, and effectiveness. Since talent, too, is driven by ambition, it has the capacity to make you either an aggressor or a victim. Skills are channeled strategically and with impeccable timing.

Know-it-all investors risk walking right into their own reflections in the mirror and shattering their self-image. Look carefully in the mirror to draw crosshairs. Discover and bond with a true friend—the sum of your internal negotiating strengths. Bond with the friend of your strengths, and eliminate the foes of any weaknesses.

Then turn the focal point to the foe—the seller across the negotiating table who's in the way of acquiring a property. This person is also leading an offensive combat maneuver, and if terms and conditions are not met, the battle is at a standstill.

Competitors are another foe. How their capital, expertise, market knowledge, reputation and relationships compare to yours provide a realistic benchmark. If the benchmark is unrealistic, then the battle is lost before it's begun. As in warfare, the opposing army, or enemy, is not your target. Instead, the enemy is an *obstacle* to reaching the objective. If the opposing team never shows up, the battle is canceled and you win! But that's hardly a realistic scenario.

Be prepared to carry the war chest through a rough obstacle course—the investment battlefield. Be sure your equipment is in peak condition before starting any maneuvers. Take the next step in the combat investor's boot camp by moving forward using your ambition transmission.

AMBITION TRANSMISSION

"Business is like riding a bicycle. Either you keep moving or you fall down."

John David Wright

A tank driver moving forward in battle while looking backward will inevitably run off the course. So will you, if moving in the wrong direction. The ambition transmission tool gauges the desire to succeed and keeps moving in the right direction—forward.

Check your P-R-N-D shifter every time you drive your ambition:

- **Procrastination (Park)**
  You are not interested in the battlefield. Lots of talk, but no plan. You probably wouldn't be reading this book if in Park. Procrastination parks the mind in a garage. The war chest is simply too heavy and bulky to move.

- **Resentment (Reverse)**
  Envy, jealousy and ill feelings endanger the combat investor's effectiveness. Looking backward for a long time generates negative energy and destructive consequences. Negative emotions are inevitable but temporary. Remember the ultimate goal is to trek forward with goals and objectives (in Drive.) War chests occasionally move backward or sideways to bypass obstacles.

- **Noncommittal (Neutral)**
  Nonresponsive, nonperforming—any mindset with a "non" prefix refers to this least utilized gear. Neutrality is battlefield indecision in the front line of fire—more dangerous than procrastination. In Neutral, an engine is unable to brake and control of the tank is precarious. Neutral is necessary only for towing. Stay out of Neutral; it's better to be in Park. Neutral should not be confused with a preparation lull, which is required when formulating an action plan. The war chest is more easily damaged or stolen in this position.

- **D**rive
  Regular (D), Low-Mid Gear (D2) and First Gear (D1)
  represent the levels of drive or "D" gears. Are you very
  ambitious (overdrive) or moderately ambitious (the lower
  gears)? Moving forward means journeying toward success.
  The forward motion in any real estate venture is propelled
  by greed and stalled by fear. In Drive, the commitment is to
  move forward, but steering and braking is part of reaching
  the target. The war chest is heading straight for battle.

The ambition transmission is designed to propel you toward the
front line. A combat-ready vehicle is made to go forward as fast as
weather and terrain will allow. Gauge the speed in accordance with
your ambition and style. Choose to work slower and longer hours,
or take more aggressive risks, driving faster toward the target.

Shifting is beneficial. Driving in reverse for a quick check on the
competition is useful. Periodically pausing in neutral prevents rash,
impulsive moves. Occasional procrastination allows you to regroup
before the next attack. And a dose of doubt sometimes inhibits
overly aggressive ambitions. But remember, constant gearshifting
damages the transmission, so choose a strategy and stay with it.
You are meant to move forward. The war chest should be mobile,
ready to move ahead to new opportunities at all times. But moving
forward is no guarantee of gaining ground. You still have to tune
your ambition transmission with the triangle of perfection, properly
aligning talent, time, and costs.

TRIANGLE OF PERFECTION: MISSION IMPOSSIBLE

Now that the war chest is towed in the right direction in boot camp,
you're almost ready for battle. In the fast-paced real estate business,
savvy buyers move quickly on attractively priced deals. Bad deals

linger in search of the greater fool. When hunting and negotiating deals, channel talent decisively using another pyramid—the project triangle. The project triangle encompasses three talent-channeling variables that are constantly at play. It's possible to secure two, but not all three, in any given combat investment effort:

- **Good and Fast**

  This type of project uses expensive deployment for quick results. This combination requires assembling ample talent and abundant resources to attack an investment in a short period. Attorneys, engineers, construction managers, investment analysts, and other development professionals instantly redirect their resources to complete an acquisition on short notice for the combat investor.

- **Good and Cheap**

  This type of project is possible when the economic climate is very uncertain and filled with desperate, motivated sellers. Good and cheap opportunities are rare in the fast-paced, information-packed real estate investment field. Good and cheap is the combat's investor's perfect shot in the sightline.

- **Fast and Cheap**
  This scenario is undesirable because a rushed, sloppy deal with limited resources inevitably leads to costly mistakes. A combat investor acts quickly and resolutely, but not at the cost of quality—in military terms, a quickly planned strike with limited resources. Very risky.

How will you be called to duty? What will be your role? How will you enter the financial battlefront? Good, fast, or cheap?

CALL TO DUTY

"I have nothing to offer but blood, toil, tears, and sweat."
Winston Churchill

It's time to move the war chest to the front line from boot camp. Are your talents and skills matched to the risk profile?

As you know, the closer you get to the investment battlefield front line, the higher the level of risk and reward and the closer to victory or defeat. Highly driven investors stand on the front line, while more conservative and passive investors play behind the lines, in combat support roles perhaps guarding war chests. These basic risk-tolerance talent profiles include:

- **Noncombatants**
  Incidental investors don't enter the battlefield. Instead, they choose to control only that real estate that's directly associated with the immediate environment—mainly private residences and small business property. Their tour of duty is to use real estate as a supplemental investment, augmenting shelter and occupation. These noncombatant investors seldom require talent beyond regular building maintenance and standard ownership responsibilities. Attempting offensive realty maneuvers are rare.

- **Supply Staff**
  Passive individual investors seek more than an owner-occupied asset. They pursue direct ownership of real estate as investment. Because management and ownership expertise is limited and such players don't aspire to make investing a full-time profession, these passive investors in a venture are frequently called the country club money (doctors, lawyers, accountants, and wealthy acquaintances). Most of them merely look to fund real estate investments but have no decision-making ambitions.

- **Weekend Warriors**
  Active investors seeking to make real estate investing a career join the front line troops to start targeting deals. Many begin as part-time players, eventually becoming full-time investors.

Although weekend warriors are not equipped for full-time duty, they are ready to jump into battle to develop talents.

- **Combat Soldiers**

  Eager rookies, these full-time investors have limited operational and development expertise. The risk tolerance is high, energized by raw work—blood, sweat and tears. The rookies have high survival rates when operating in friendly territory with local market expertise and guerrilla warfare tactics. Combat soldiers apply talents close to home and hire support talent such as attorneys, accountants, and leasing agents.

- **Intelligence Units**

  These are hired talent in the behind-the-scenes arena of espionage. These investors research and analyze companies, avoiding direct contact with the target. The ranks include Wall Street analysts, financial consulting firms, brokerage companies, and pension fund advisors providing regional and national intelligence and reconnaissance. Appraisers, local brokers, and counselors deal with intelligence in the immediate area.

- **Officers**

  Developers are the ultimate combat investors, fully dedicating talent to operational tasks. These are the front line officers, making command decisions and marshaling troops and resources on the battlefront. Officers take on the highest level of responsibility and risk.

Now you've graduated boot camp by reviewing your ambitions, talents, resources, and risk preferences. You know your rank and serial number. Be true to yourself. Stay focused on what personally suits you. That said, what's your investment style? What kind of war machine are you?

CHAPTER 5

ARMED AND DANGEROUS: YOU'RE A WAR MACHINE

"The character of a president colors his entire administration."
Clark M. Clifford

SABER RATTLING

Draw weapons to collect your realty riches! Democracy leaders and dictators alike realize the importance of parading their weapons, waving their sticks, beating their drums, and otherwise pounding their chests. One-upmanship is a time-honored practice. Imagine Red Square or North Korea without an annual military parade or Western powers without any air shows. Weapons project authority and saber rattling deters wars, as demonstrated by the Cold War.

Combat investors, too, display their financial power, authority, durability, reliability, and leadership acumen to garner respect from the competition. But the combat investor also is ready to strike with these weapons. Just as weapons systems with computer circuitry require constant upgrading, the combat investor's attitude requires adjustment in accordance with the latest technological innovations.

Here the military arena provides constructive parallels. Test drones function as trial balloons, which allow new ideas to be tried out without committing too many resources to a project. Reconnaissance drones go ahead of the forces to provide real-time video images of the surroundings to help troops avoid surprises and traps. Such innovations will inevitably tweak real estate investing psychology, as both seller and buyer gain more knowledge of each other's intentions.

Weaponry mishaps also teach the combat investor what to avoid. Like the early Vietnam-era M-16 rifles, technologically sophisticated weapons are effective under ideal testing conditions but fail in the field. A good design in the wrong application proves disastrous for both the warrior and the real estate investor.

What is the preferred attack style for filling the war chest? Do you use a peashooter for practice or prefer to wipe out the target with a bazooka? Are you a tactical or strategic investor?

- **Tactical**
  This is a hands-on approach to investing. You're always touching the war chest. The tactical combat investor battles in familiar territory and assumes individual responsibility, striving for complete command of a limited body of information. Tactical investors are "do-it-yourselfers" whose physical and skill set limitations permit small-scale investments only.

- **Strategic**
  Handling the war chest is a group effort. Strategic investors' larger organizations are armed with multiple disciplines such as in-house accounting, management, acquisitions, dispositions, brokerage, and other vital functions. Such capabilities enable larger portfolios with local, regional, and national-scale operations.

SMART DEPLOYMENT

Talent is useless unless deployed productively. The war chest is an empty box. To determine how to apply talent to a project ask, "How should the combat investor (talent) deploy weapons and ammunition (capital) to reach a target (project) with the most effective strike (profit)?"

As choices are made about what ammunition to deploy in what quantities and distances, investors tend to fit weapon archetypes such as the bunker, the helicopter, the tank, the B-52 bomber, the jet fighter, the stealth bomber, the submarine, the aircraft carrier, and the drone.

Some weapons, such as missiles, rockets, and bullets, are not applicable. These arms are unmanned, single-use, and single-purpose. Would you want to be a one-shot wonder?

Review the tactical and strategic attributes in the following weapons system catalog and then decide what fits your real estate investment style.

WEAPONS SYSTEM CATALOG

BUNKER

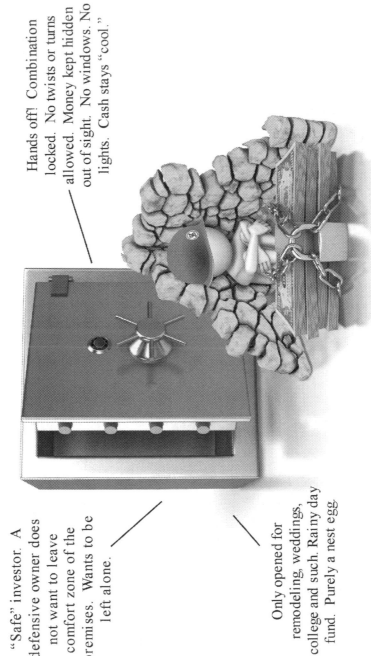

Hands off! Combination locked. No twists or turns allowed. Money kept hidden out of sight. No windows. No lights. Cash stays "cool."

"Safe" investor. A defensive owner does not want to leave comfort zone of the premises. Wants to be left alone.

Only opened for remodeling, weddings, college and such. Rainy day fund. Purely a nest egg.

- **Bunker**

  Above or below grade, the bunker is an effective
  self-defense weapon, which is heavily armored and
  purely defensive. It has no capacity to expand beyond
  the immediate surroundings. Bunkers are tactical and
  reactive—the only stationary weapon system in the catalog.

  Combat Investor Profile

  o overwhelming majority of investors (homeowner,
     building and land-owning businessperson, corporate
     manufacturer, distributor, etc.)
  o views real estate as ancillary to business or basic shelter
  o no desire to expand holdings beyond immediate needs
  o limited knowledge of markets; requires hiring
     professionals

  Goal

  Asset Preservation.

  Reconnaissance

  The starting point for every investor, bunker is the
  birthplace. If you want to leave your shell, then come out of
  the bunker.

HELICOPTER

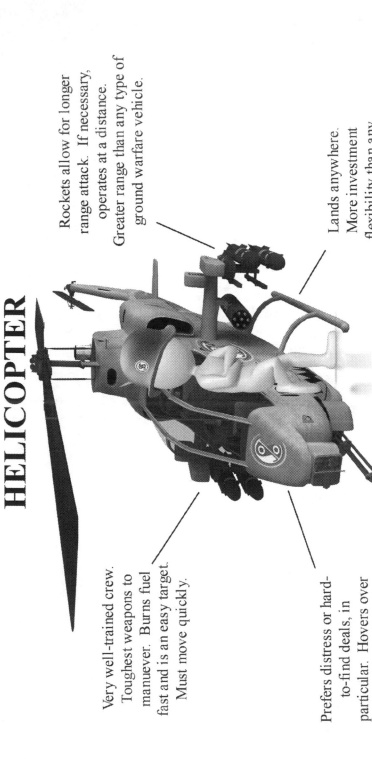

Rockets allow for longer range attack. If necessary, operates at a distance. Greater range than any type of ground warfare vehicle.

Lands anywhere. More investment flexibility than any other investor type.

Very well-trained crew. Toughest weapons to manuever. Burns fuel fast and is an easy target. Must move quickly.

Prefers distress or hard-to-find deals, in particular. Hovers over investments other find too challenging.

- **Helicopter**

The attack helicopter is one of the military's most versatile weapons platforms. The profile is difficult to spot during sudden raids. The attack chopper lands in very tight spaces that are impossible for most types of equipment. Flying in all types of terrain at fast speeds and heavily armed with machine guns, rockets and other offensive gear, the chopper is a ground support weapon with few equals. Hampered by limited range, this aircraft is most effective for quick attacks near the operating base.

Combat Investor Profile

o small, elite firm staffed by highly-trained thrill-seekers "eating what they kill"
o fiercely independent, primed for quick action on complicated missions (workouts, turnaround deals and value-add ventures)
o pursue profitability from individual performance rather than wages (except clerical staff)
o advised by brokers, appraisers, and other professionals offering market intelligence
o deals pursued are seldom on the market or conversely abandoned; easier deals left to others
o utilize stealth and surprise, staying close to the ground in localized market only
o funded by entrepreneurial private venture capital
o avoids an opportunity if competitors have already spotted value, judged as being too late in the game
o bid low and usually pay cash for a quick close

Goal

Highly profitable deals. Transaction volume is not a top priority.

Reconnaissance

The attack helicopter is highly focused and always nimble, landing on only very specialized properties that others perceive as too difficult. These investors are very close to their asset base for maximum coverage with intense management. After value is created, these entrepreneurs sell to other investors that seek less risk. They are clearly tactical investors in both equipment and timelines.

TANK

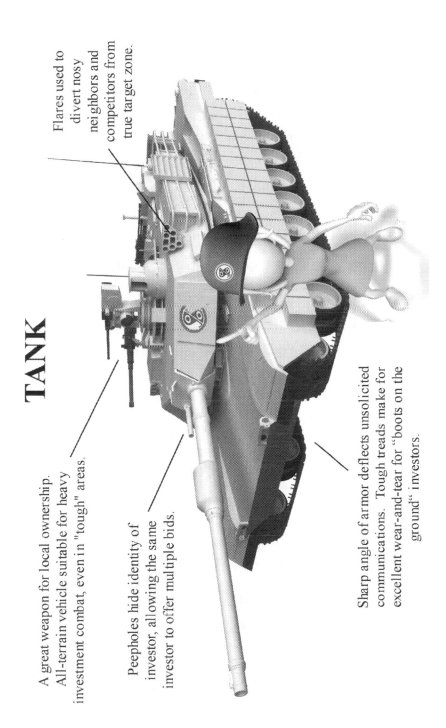

Flares used to divert nosy neighbors and competitors from true target zone.

A great weapon for local ownership. All-terrain vehicle suitable for heavy investment combat, even in "tough" areas.

Peepholes hide identity of investor, allowing the same investor to offer multiple bids.

Sharp angle of armor deflects unsolicited communications. Tough treads make for excellent wear-and-tear for "boots on the ground" investors.

- **Tank**

A cautious, slow-moving and decisive tactical weapon. The tank is a heavily armored vehicle attacking each target at a close distance within conventional artillery range. A tank participates in the heart of battle and is designed for the front line.

Combat Investor Profile

- o private investor, developer—usually an individual or family-owned enterprise
- o part-time or full-time
- o hands-on approach to operations
- o heavily camouflaged—local player blends in with immediate surroundings
- o easy to spot out of its environment (short hunting range)
- o avoids outside investors and partners
- o completes one transaction at a time; not spread too thin
- o handles all aspects of the negotiation and closing process
- o many transactions are off-the-market deals made through neighborhood contacts
- o avoids bidding wars and working with outside brokers, unless project is extremely close to existing holdings (part of an assemblage)
- o reliable for closing a single transaction
- o uses instinct rather than relying on sophisticated cash flow modeling
- o Renaissance man with diversified skills—management, repairs, and maintenance

Goal

To grow at a comfortable pace within personal limitations.

Reconnaissance

Given its slower speed, large size, and local camouflage markings, investments unfamiliar to the tank expose it to vulnerability. Heavy artillery and ordinance make it useful for acquiring a specific target with high certainty. Despite its easily detectable size and noise level, the tank is the best on-the-ground weapon for smaller, management-intensive projects.

JET FIGHTER

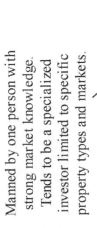

Manned by one person with strong market knowledge. Tends to be a specialized investor limited to specific property types and markets.

Sleek design helps cut through unnecessary trivia. A decisive and direct communicator seldom wastes time.

Carries enough munitions for a round trip on a specific investment attack. Greater geographic transaction range than any ground vehicle or helicopter.

- **Jet Fighter**

The jet fighter is an offensive tactical weapon usually manned by one to two people. It has wider territorial coverage than the tank and gets to its targets very quickly. The jet fighter carries a large variety of payload for different types of attacks but only for shorter-range missions.

Combat Investor Profile

o full-time private investor, small corporation, or family-owned business
o covers a wider range of markets, usually with one-day driving distance
o wants control, but partners are optional
o completes one transaction at a time
o greater workload requires more delegation
o lacks a full-time market presence for on-the-ground intelligence so buys listed properties and works through brokers
o not necessarily a local, so pays higher prices
o moves more quickly and aggressively than local players
o flies by radar using sophisticated investment analysis based on cash flow modeling

Goal

To grow faster by expanding geographic horizons.

Reconnaissance

The jet fighter is the sports car of the weapons world.
This tactical weapon covers a greater territory than any
land-based alternative. However, the jet fighter demands
more maintenance and a larger support crew, necessitating
more delegation of responsibilities. It's an excellent
entrepreneurial weapon providing a wider range, while
controlling territorial gains on a smaller scale.

STEALTH FIGHTER

"High flying" investors avoid detection. Quiet and only speaks when collecting market information. Asks questions, but seldom gives answers.

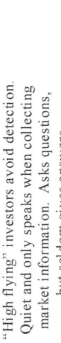

Nearly impossible to identify markings, even on the ground. Interchangeable identity morphs quickly, depending upon investment transaction and circumstances.

Manned by one person with secret identity and role. Keeps everyone guessing. Is this an investor, a broker, a lawyer, a seller?

- **Stealth Fighter**

The stealth fighter is an extremely small, agile, and speedy tactical weapon and intelligence-gathering aircraft that flies virtually undetected. It provides an on-demand support role for strategic missions.

Combat Investor Profile

o individual—the "deal guy" with possibly a small team
o indirect investor, usually uses a broker or other intermediary
o well camouflaged; investment intentions (brokering or buying) unclear
o opportunistic; may work for firms of various types and sizes but ultimately works for oneself
o highly educated and sophisticated; utilizes state-of-the-art information collection technologies for extensive research
o handles negotiation process but delegates other responsibilities to co-investors
o not geographically constrained; executes investment partner's preferences
o belongs to numerous trade groups and is constantly networking

Goal

To find the prime opportunity missed by others.

Reconnaissance

The lightly-armed stealth fighter is a most effective weapon system, which utilizes technology to locate outstanding investment opportunities and define precise funding objectives. It "cherry picks" deals (buys the best; ignores the rest). Relies almost entirely on outside weapons support to scout the front line and close on the prime opportunities in the marketplace.

B-52 BOMBER

Solid, combat-proven platform. Carpet bombing mass marketing works! Kept up to date for deal making with upgrades to electronic and direct marketing solicitations.

Seeking high visibility, thriving on publicity. Large tail and fuselage provides ideal signage and advertising opportunities. Acts like a brokerage firm.

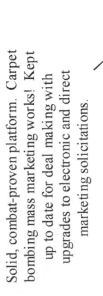

Needs large crew to man investment campaigns. Sales force "pilots" run the show while office staff provides heavy support.

- **B-52 Bomber**

In service since 1952, the B-52 bomber is a US Air Force workhorse. It carries multiple weapons (cruise missiles, laser bombs, and conventional warheads) and even launches smaller aircraft. An enormous, versatile, reliable, and strategic weapons platform with huge fuel capacity, the B-52 bomber flies anywhere, anytime. The typical mission for this classic "carpet bombing" aircraft is the dispersing of multiple warheads over a large, scattered area. With its high capacity, this strategic bomber delivers tactical support.

Combat Investor Profile

- o   seeks a high profile and visibility on a regional and/or national basis
- o   an organization staffed with a variety of disciplines and skill sets, typically a non-public entity in a central location
- o   requires large workforce for heavy workload, top-heavy with marketing personnel
- o   direct investor pursues larger portfolios and market share
- o   occasionally reinforced with growth-oriented, passive capital
- o   a marketing machine, using all means necessary to promote investment programs (cold calls, mass mailings, internet and newspaper ads, TV, and radio spots)
- o   known for offering multiple bids on a large scale
- o   "fast at the trigger," prioritizing volume of transactions as key measure of success

Goal

To build wealth ASAP and to abide by "Always Be Closing" rule.

Reconnaissance

The B-52 covers an enormously wide range of investment opportunities. Accuracy and precision are overshadowed by pure transaction volume. Designed to acquire and market properties but not equipped to operate or set up a beachhead. Great takeover candidate for larger organizations.

SUBMARINE

Looks simple on the outside, but is loaded with complex equipment hidden from view. Completely self-contained and independent. This investor typifies a secluded wealthy family than shuns publicity.

Periscopes see, but can't be seen. Large investment vessel shows only a small footprint to avoid detection. Low profile, but financially highly armed.

Stays submerged, except when deal hunting. Whereabouts unknown, but when this investor surfaces, everyone pays attention as the chances of a successful transaction escalate instantly.

- **Submarine**

The nuclear submarine is the military's secretive all-or-nothing system. Lethal and extremely expensive, this nearly invisible weapon is always on the move. Armed with nuclear warheads, it was designed for the last resort attack but has also been used for patrolling and the occasional rescue mission at sea. Nuclear power provides over a two-month long patrol in all parts of the globe. The sub is a strategic weapon with maximum strike capabilities.

Combat Investor Profile

- seasoned money, private investors, typically wealthy families
- surfaces only on occasion
- all dough, no show; money is no object but seldom flaunts wealth
- attracts off-the-market properties; requires anonymity
- negotiations handled through attorneys, brokers, and other intermediaries
- purchases any property type with net lease properties (for example, 1031 tax-deferred) the most common; families want safe, long-term yield for estate planning
- occasionally invests with stealth partner

Goal

To protect assets and preserve net worth.

Reconnaissance

This self-contained weapon system is shrouded in secrecy. Neither seen nor heard, it's a hunter with a deadly sting. This most effective and least understood investor type has enough staying power to outlast the competition.

CARRIER

Typically a publicly-traded company, this investor has large and clear markings necessary for raising money.

Costs more than any other military vessel. Stays afloat as long as profits do. Once outdated, it's sold for scrap value. Must constantly be on deal patrol to survive.

All major financial resources on deck. Easy for analysts and shareholders to openly observe. Thrives on predictablity, so no sharp turns or maneuvers. Steady on course.

- **Aircraft Carrier**

An aircraft carrier is the most expensive and most massive show of force on the planet, a floating city surrounded by a protective fleet of destroyers, cruisers, and other types of war vessels. An aircraft carrier battle group is made to be seen and heard—a body-building show. The carrier is an all-purpose tool being both tactical (firepower is delivered by short-range fighter planes) and strategic (reaches all areas of the globe accompanied by entire battle group).

Combat Investor Profile

- a large public or private institution (REIT, pension fund, insurance company, major corporation)
- the "800- pound gorilla" in the room
- no geographic limits
- seasoned professionals operate as full-service owner/ managers with large staff
- most renowned player in the marketplace
- aggregator—buys smaller and/or growth companies (likely to acquire successful jet fighters, B-52 bombers, or hire stealth bombers)
- sees every listed deal in the marketplace
- analyzed and studied by the media and real estate research organizations
- every move is clearly visible

Goal

To capture market share based on publicly-stated investment objectives.

Reconnaissance

This is the top weapon in the military food chain. Like the submarine, the aircraft carrier is a fully self-contained weapon system. It boasts unlimited range but requires high maintenance. Physical presence is its greatest strength and weakness. The aircraft carrier is subjected to espionage from other weapons groups.

DRONE

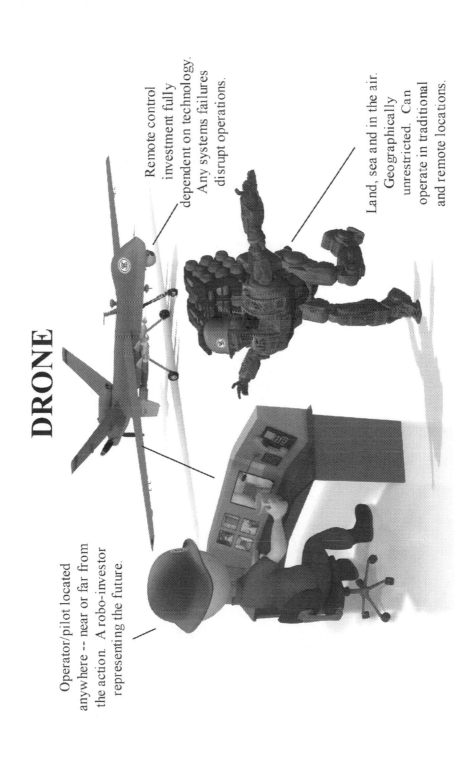

Remote control investment fully dependent on technology. Any systems failures disrupt operations.

Land, sea and in the air. Geographically unrestricted. Can operate in traditional and remote locations.

Operator/pilot located anywhere -- near or far from the action. A robo-investor representing the future.

- **Drone**

The drone is the future, the most effective method of striking a target without risking valuable manpower. It is highly mobile, is easy to set up, has a low cost per incident, and is produced on a mass scale with no personal casualties, just equipment losses. The opponent never sees who is delivering the target. The drone transports anywhere via unmanned aircraft, ships, and infantry robots. Drone operators are safely out of harm's way from the target. Drone warfare is the closest thing to a deadly video game. Although not occupied by a pilot, the drone is classified as a manned weapon since it's reusable and in full control by a remote pilot.

Combat Investor Profile

o   the program and day trader of the real estate industry
o   any size firm, small or large real estate operation, since set up costs are minimal; a stand-alone operation or as part of a large multiplatform real estate investment organization
o   an automated solution to real estate investing
o   no geographic limits and follows the information flow, avoiding any dead zones where market data is limited or unavailable
o   every move is geared toward program trading and investing with limited flexibility to go beyond the predetermined complete investment formulas

Goal

Conquer deals that are within the predetermined investment formula.

Reconnaissance

With the drone, the operator/pilot is removed directly from the physical action, which is a dangerous investment format if the operator loses touch with reality and ignores assets outside the trading model. Furthermore, investment nuances and changing areas may not be properly analyzed unless the investor does independent research over and above the reporting services. As seasoned investors already know, real estate ownership is far from a programmatic activity; any capable operator is close to the assets on a regular basis. That said, many components of the drone investment model should be incorporated into real estate investing, especially relating to research.

In summary, these tactical and strategic weapons operate synergistically. For example, the jet and stealth fighter identifies opportunities for the submarine and aircraft carrier. The tank sports excellent relationships with local bunkers. The helicopter teams up with the drone for a quick acquisition opportunity requiring excellent research with strong ground support. As technology and military tactics evolve, these systems will collaborate even more efficiently. New weapons systems will emerge as well. You will find more creative ways to cram your war chest.

These weapon systems archetypes only serve as guidelines. You'll ultimately determine which of these systems work for you. You're now a war machine and it's time to hunt for targets.

CHAPTER 6

LOCK ON TARGET: GETTING PREMISES IN THE CROSSHAIRS

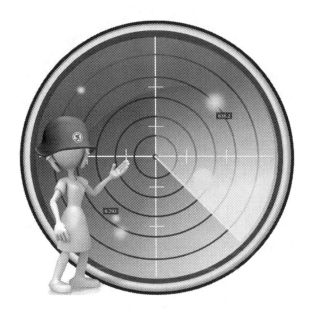

"I'm easy. Put me in an interesting location with good people and I'm there."

Jane Curtin

RADAR LOVE

"Location, location, location" is the age-old adage that still describes a very important and fretted-over factor in real estate site selection for your battlefield. Good intelligence solves this investment battlefield quandary. Investors mistakenly believe that hot markets with quickly rising values are the best battlefields for finding easy money. This misconception eclipses many other factors considered before investing and building an empire. Unless you've tapped some source of superior intelligence, by the time such areas are discovered, it's too late. To find the perfect direction for investments, tune your risk tolerance compass and then direct the capital and talent to a true north comfort point.

What sort of want ad would you post to find that perfect location?

> *Wanted! A location situated in a gateway coastal, 24-hour city restricted by high barriers to entry. City has to be a full-employment center with continued growth prospects, pollution-free, crime-free, mild climate, and friendly residents. A community offering low property taxes, excellent medical, and educational, cultural, and recreational amenities. Site to be directly linked to fiber optic communication lines as well as a reliable power grid. Should be close to public transportation, offer ample parking, and link to walking paths with excellent ingress/ egress. Most importantly—priced to sell.*

Good luck in getting any responses for this perfect-deal ad! Prepare your weapons systems for a long and drawn-out search for a nonexistent target.

Although important, location is not necessarily the end-all factor in real estate selection. Combat investors earn handsome rewards in ostensibly less desirable areas throughout the country, once locational risks are properly assessed. Since every site offers unique pricing dynamics (sometimes even subsidies), pinpointing the right location requires a blend of art and science. And choosing the location—the deal battlefield—the combat investor's real motivations should be separated from ideal conditions.

Location radar helps the combat investor navigate through variable factors to determine what investment areas truly make sense. The most significant variables are positioned closer to the center of the screen with the less important closer to the outer edges. These variables include:

- supply and demand imbalance
- government presence
- diversification
- low crime rate
- technology/communications
- medical/biomedical facilities
- easy access to public transportation
- academia/ education
- job-growth and income level of workforce
- barriers to entry
- climate
- competitive price

There are no cut-and-dried rules. Each location is analyzed individually. Fortunes are made in obscure markets with less-than-ideal property types. Investment battlefield locations fall into one of two categories—tactical or strategic.

- **Tactical Locations**
  Combat investors seeking tactical investment locations choose not only project economics but make lifestyle choices. Tactical investors take into consideration family ties, socioeconomic interests, climate preferences, travel time, and distance. Their selection methodology is subjective, based mostly on convenience. The war chest stays close to home.

- **Strategic Locations**
  Strategic investing is driven by hard facts and pure
  economics. The selected locations meet profit targets,
  requiring investors to journey greater distances for optimal
  yields. The war chest is very mobile.

Choosing an investment location is more often art than a science,
just as when an experienced commander uses survival instincts
to find the target. Is the investment decision tactical or strategic?
Where are you confident that you'll win? Local, infill, or
farmland? Single asset or a portfolio of properties? Scattered
nationally or concentrated locally? Battlefields abound, limited
only by your imagination. To triumph, follow the appropriate rules
of engagement and stay within the right attack zones.

RULES AND ZONES OF ATTACK

"Few rich men own their property; the property owns them."
Robert Ingersoll

Once the chosen investment battlefield is on your radar, decide what type of properties to target. Wandering aimlessly in search of deals is akin to cross-eyed target practice. You know where to go with the war chest, but what type of booty do you stuff inside? Consider all types of premises (either one asset or several assets) you could conquer such as a residence, a shopping center, an office building, a lodging facility, vacant land, or an apartment complex. How large? Should it be an operating property, new construction, or rehab? When making your decision, follow these three combat investor rules relating to timing:

1. **The Submarine Rule**

    "It's a hard fight with a short stick."
    Chief Officer Steward Dogan

    Carry enough resources and cash reserves to power ownership through very deep waters for the long journey to profit. Like a submarine, be prepared to stay submerged for months. Once out on the high seas, it's tough to refuel. And don't borrow too much for operations. If you carry too much debt, you become the target, moving slowly and potentially sinking in red ink due to too heavy of a financial load. Be careful. Otherwise, your war chest will sink and be rediscovered by someone else.

2. **The Rocket Rule**

    "I know this defies the law of *gravity*, but *I never studied* law!"

    Bugs Bunny, Warner Bros.

Be realistic. What goes up quickly comes down even quicker. It takes much more power to launch a rocket than to crash it. Rocket launches are expensive and plagued by high failure rates. The rocket is only in the clear when it reaches the upper atmosphere. Don't expect stratospheric investment returns with stellar appreciation unless you're a real estate rocket scientist! Stick with more down-to-earth projects touting realistic yields and achievable goals. Once property values climb through the atmosphere, move quickly and sell! The war chest takes more effort to carry than to drop.

3. **The Sniper Rule**

"We are built to conquer environment, solve problems, achieve goals, and we find no real satisfaction or happiness in life without obstacles to conquer and goals to achieve."

Maxwell Maltz

Once you've determined the property types and markets—and secured sufficient cash with realistic hopes—choose your target carefully. Like the sniper in the woods, wait for a clear shot at the target. Don't expose yourself or you'll lose your chance. You seldom capture more than a couple of opportunities to acquire the targeted premises. Be patient. Don't waste precious time and resources. Make an investment on your terms not on theirs. Careless snipers become targets. Grab and hide your booty inside the war chest quickly, otherwise it's gone.

Now you understand how timing plays in the target selection process and what type of weapon system you want to be. Based upon your war machine, choose between tactical and strategic targets for defining the investment holding period:

- **Tactical Hold**

  All projects with short-term durations (five years or less) are tactical targets. The combat investor usually has little interest in such premises after value-creation (completion of construction, rehab, and acquisition repositioning). In this case, you're a merchant builder pursuing quick profit. This is a grab-and-run war chest that's light and maneuverable.

  The most common type of tactical project target is the single family home "flip"—a quick turnover of cash. The combat investor, often a handyman, spends six months to a year to complete a rehab. Tactical targets also include new construction properties that will be sold upon completion and premises converted for alternative use (for example, warehouse to loft apartments).

- **Strategic Hold**

  Most real estate projects are strategic since real estate investing is illiquid. Such ventures require multi-year holding periods with seasoned technical expertise and sufficient cash on hand to weather any problems. The strategic hold is essentially a heavier, bulkier way to build a war chest, requiring more time and planning to move.

Nearly every type of real estate investment falls into the strategic timeline. No quick money here . . . just hard work, persistence, and dedication.

THE RIGHT PROPERTY TYPES

As in the battlefield, investors quickly react to changing conditions—good or bad. The war chest needs the right mix of goodies. On occasion, unexpected conditions force investment reevaluation. For instance, long-term holding plans might shift to selling an asset because of higher prices resulting from lower interest rates. If the opposite occurs, tactical investors are forced to hold on to properties longer because buyers evaporate as was the case with the Great Recession. Timing works for and against you; it never hurts to be smart *and* lucky!

Let's cover property types for a war chest, keeping in mind timing, ownership expertise, financial resources, geographic constraints, and transaction size. And when deciding on the optimal investment blend, many common sense rules apply, such as the smaller the project, the more direct management time needed. What type of properties should you chase with your war machine?

Again, single-family housing is the most common target, followed by the four food groups of commercial real estate: apartment, industrial, office, and retail assets. Lodging is often added as an extra category. These more popular project types are summarized as follows:

1. Housing

"I think that there will always be a need for Housing and Urban Development."

Alphonso Jackson

Housing is a war chest with bedrooms, a safe bet if done right. For the combat investor, the house is literally the home base. Homeownership trumps other real estate purchases because it's not only an investment but also a source of shelter and security, savings, status, lifestyle, and community amenities. If the purchase is to be used for shelter, it should be held for at least five years. Home buyers should set aside about a third of their annual income for mortgage, realty taxes, and insurance payments.

To homeowners, buying and selling residential units is the least sophisticated investment and a logical choice for beginner investors. Local market research is easy to do, and there are several purchase formats: directly from owner, via broker, auction, short sale, or bank foreclosure.

In the United States, deduction of interest rate payments provides an attractive tax break, and the stability of homeowner communities makes purchasing attractive. The days of uncontrolled appreciation are gone because too many lenders and homeowners invested in their premises when property values were overinflated and fueled by speculation. Owning one's home, however, continues to provide a steady hedge against inflation and the accompanying rising interest rates. Some quick rules-of-thumb on home affordability pricing include two and a half times your annual income or a price-to-annual-rent ratio of 20 times or less.

Strike Zones

- o   Homeownership cheaper than renting, depending upon markets.
- o   Hands-on operations only; too costly for professional management.
- o   Quick turnaround; typical "flip" cycle of six months or less.
- o   Steady appreciation under normal circumstances; rapid appreciation under speculative conditions; poor or negative appreciation during recessions and tight lending cycles.
- o   Fixer-uppers provide steady profits and ease of entry/exit into the market if completed on a one-at-a-time basis in the appropriate market cycle.
- o   Abundant vacant land and rehab residences provide nearly limitless opportunities.
- o   Manufactured housing and ground rent income offer steady profits with minimal risk.
- o   Infill, urban land with restrictive zoning, protects the profitability of this asset class by limiting new supply.
- o   Federal tax credits available to first-time buyers.
- o   Foreclosure property speculation is rewarding but risky.

Danger Zones

o Expect realistic appreciation mirrored by inflation—the traditional thinking.
o Speculative investing contributes to false profit expectations and leads to housing bubbles.
o Owner-occupied housing should be considered shelter, not a trading commodity.
o Minimal barriers to entry during loose financial markets conditions allow anyone with scant resources and financials to enter the game, leading to over-speculation.
o Shallow scattered housing markets are extremely competitive and diversified.
o Occasionally bidding wars produce homeowners willing to pay emotional premiums that are less related to profitability.

Plan of Attack

o Be prepared for a new job as a small-scale landlord. You're the manager, janitor, tenant representative, and owner all in one—a 24/7 responsibility.
o Avoid easy-to-build markets with ample land supply and limited development restrictions.
o Follow the jobs where people can afford to pay rent (if necessary) or increased home prices. Rising home prices are found in higher job growth markets, so invest near major public/private institutions such as hospitals, schools, and governmental facilities.
o Develop and invest close to public transportation. Take advantage of new benefits offered by communities in promoting smart development.

○ Exercise caution with condominiums, especially with smaller properties. Perform extensive due diligence on owner litigation, deferred maintenance, hidden assessments, and other pitfalls associated with this ownership form. Small condo projects are often rife with conflicts, since a condo neighbor is also a partner. Professional management is not affordable on this small scale. Ask yourself this. Would you want to be in a foxhole with your condominium owners?

○ Rising material costs favor buying and holding existing properties. Be very selective with new construction.

Reconnaissance

○ National Association Home Builders is the trade group representing homebuilders.

○ National Associations of Realtors®, the largest real estate brokers trade group and lobby organization in the country.

2. Apartments/Multifamily

"In a booming market, sellers can be choosers."
Amir Efrati

Apartment buildings are larger war chests filled with even more bedrooms. Welcome to the multiple bedroom business! These property types are the next logical step for single-family home investors, being in the same general asset class. Multifamily management and leasing expertise is readily available, and smaller scale investors control operations and act as handymen. Rental growth is mostly tied to inflation and enjoys the highest occupancy of any commercial property type. According to the US Census Bureau, more than 36 million rental units are in service.

This asset class is tougher to build because of construction costs, zoning restrictions, and land affordability. Except in the most expensive markets, tenants are seldom willing to pay the premiums necessary to justify new construction.

Strike Zones

o   Smaller households are becoming prevalent, increasing demand for these types of units.
o   Smaller units require less sophisticated management expertise.
o   Increased mortgage rates and tight credit hamper ownership affordability.
o   This property type fulfills a basic human need—shelter.
o   Baby boomer demographics support renter growth as more people choose ownership-free lifestyles and carefree living for their retirement years.
o   A tremendous amount of diverse inventory is found in a host of locations.
o   Inflation and rent adjustments are more frequent and flexible—weekly, monthly, and annual.
o   Senior housing (independent living) requires intensive management expertise but promises higher profits.
o   Higher interest rates and declining home prices favor renting over owning.

Danger Zones

- o Condominium units offer less control of ownership and are subject to the operational whims of the condo board.
- o Ease of entry into this property sector assures intense competition from all types of investors.
- o Low interest rate and liberal lending policy cycles favor homeownership.
- o More management-intensive and requires regular contact with renters.
- o When tenant preferences change, an inappropriate unit mix penalizes large or small units.
- o Frequent tenant rollover is costly.

Plan of Attack

- o Older properties in excellent locations offer better price competition protection against newer, more luxurious units that charge higher rents to justify construction costs.
- o Avoid new construction, unless markets are extremely tight and/or condo-conversion is reducing existing inventory.
- o Target locations compete against less affordable condominium and single-family housing—rental increases are easier to collect.
- o Choose unfriendly housing markets with vexing rules and regulations imposed by anti-growth constituents. Supply constraints will protect investments.
- o Student housing investments present favorable alternative apartment rental opportunities. Parental

guarantees and annual leases improve operational control. Buy near campus, within walking distance of facilities.

Reconnaissance

o National Apartment Association and National Multifamily Housing Council are the leading trade groups in the multifamily sector.

3. **Retail/Shopping Centers**

"The new shopping malls make possible the synthesis of all consumer activities, not least of which are shopping, flirting with objects, idle wandering, and all the permutations of these."

Jean Baudrillard

Shopping centers properties are war chests stuffed with lots of traffic lights inside. Retail premises are more location-driven than any other commercial property type. Well-located shopping centers outperform the markets, providing imperative consumer spending (groceries, toiletries, clothing, and work supplies). Retail is directly related to job growth and discretionary spending. The mall is the New Age town square and will remain a desirable socializing venue and excursion destination, also complimenting online sales. Neighborhood shopping centers, preferably grocery-anchored, perform optimally in urban and suburban infill communities. For ancillary locations, rent growth is extremely elastic—more of a commodity play. Unless retail properties are in fortress locations, "big box," "power," and "malls" are becoming forbidden industry vocabulary.

Strike Zones

- o Location, location, location. This is the most site-driven asset class, requiring high-traffic counts with ease of accessibility.
- o Retail requires disciplined development, as retailers drive demand for space (unlike industrial properties built as "spec").
- o Fortress retail properties reinforce community centers—a neighborhood anchor.
- o A variety of acquisition opportunities include mandatory shopping (food and drug stores) and entertainment/social shopping (lifestyle and fashion).
- o Retail development acts as the focal point of successful urban mixed-use projects, allowing housing and office development to gravitate to this sector.
- o This property type is a barnacle, enabling attachment to the residential sector.
- o Credit tenants with strong sales per square foot assure continued success.

Danger Zones

- o Cycles are tied to consumer spending. Rising interest rates and lagging consumer confidence dampen performance.
- o Technology is propagating brick-and-click shopping online.

- o Consumer spending habits are fickle. Changing tastes directly impact performance when the tenant mix is inappropriate.
- o Rising energy costs affect discretionary income and driving habits, as with the lodging industry but on a smaller scale.

Plan of Attack

- o Location is tied to shopping convenience and access, so there's a strong outlook for retail properties in dense urban infill sites. Follow the rooftops.
- o Performance figures, including sales per square foot and traffic counts, should be reviewed, and subtle changes in activities noted.
- o Older, below-market rented shopping centers are protected against new construction competition. In infill locations, even obsolete designs can be expanded and retrofitted.
- o Parking ratios and traffic patterns are shifting as urban centers emphasize public transportation and pedestrian traffic.
- o Seek properties with diversified tenant mix, keeping a balanced rent roll with minimal leasing exposure in any given year.

Reconnaissance

International Council of Shopping Centers is the single source of this industry. Covers it all. The one stop shop. This organization also has very active local chapters.

4. Industrial/Warehouse

"Simplicity is the ultimate form of sophistication."
Leonardo Da Vinci

Industrial assets are war chests with high ceilings and plenty of storage room. This important property sector incorporates the widest range of subcategories including manufacturing, warehousing/transfer, storage, distribution, refrigerated storage, maintenance facilities, research and development, and flex office. Industrial properties are either leased or spec. Leased projects are built-to-suit for a specific user, at times structured as a sale-leaseback ownership format. New construction industrials are speculative, as smaller and mid-size tenants rarely sign leases until project completion.

This sector is a consistently solid performer, in line with the overall economy. Cash flowing warehouse properties in major water, rail, highway, and airport hubs rank at the top of the food chain. Like other commercial space, industrial space is a commodity play generating profits through very competitive prices and terms, as compared to similar projects and locations.

Strike Zones

- Upgraded or redeveloped older warehouse space offers infill opportunity.
- This sector's defensive characteristics and high yields attract investors.
- Quick construction cycle allows supply and demand to stay in check.

o   Typical warehouse space requires minimum retrofit costs on re-leasing.

o   Management is minimal, as most leases are net of operating costs and taxes.

Danger Zone

o   Tend to be owner-occupant properties, with the exception of strategic distribution areas.

o   More specialized buildings (for example, refrigerated warehouses) fetch greater yields but carry higher re-leasing risks and are expensive to construct and maintain.

o   Low-tenant count vacant buildings require extremely strong leasing teams. Such all-or-nothing lease cycles are not appropriate for investors with shallow pockets.

o   Rent growth is disappointing, as new inventory appears on a regular basis in this short development cycle.

o   Improved logistics technologies tighten the supply chain, reducing multiple mid-level distribution channels.

Plan of Attack

o   Start small. Large portfolios are difficult to assemble. Availability is limited, as owner-occupants have a hold on many of the markets.

o   Industrial condos are suitable for owner-occupied smaller tenants.

- o Office/warehouse ranks as the most popular and easy to manage/lease property type, followed by R&D/manufacturing.
- o Climbing land values are forcing developers to rezone industrial land for residential use in hot markets. Nice problem.
- o Stay close to proven strategic locations.
- o Demand for large-scale manufacturing is likely to remain in check as the United States faces stiff competition from foreign industry.

Reconnaissance

- o Commercial Real Estate Development Association reaches developers, owners, and investors in industrial and office properties.
- o Society of Industrial Realtors. The leading industrial real estate brokerage trade group.

5. Office

"People ignore design that ignores people."
Frank Chimero

Office properties are war chests crammed with furniture wrapped by wires and electronics. One of the most challenging property types to invest in, office space is less critical space usage, as more and more work is done at home and online. Location is less important than in the past, and tenant rollover/re-leasing costs are enormous. In many parts of the country, absolute office rents are actually lower than twenty years ago!

Yet this asset class appears to be making a comeback. Concessions are burning off. There is even some real rent growth and increased earnings. Consequently, office properties will slowly gain traction in those markets with higher barriers to entry. Most of their success is redirected to downtown 24-hour city markets with job growth. Suburban assets in isolated campus settings farther from urban cores are tough sells.

Strike Zones

- o Prime, well-let long-lease premises are still attracting significant investment flows and offices remain the primary sector for investors.
- o Markets with revitalizing downtowns are ideal, particularly where older office space has been lost to apartment conversions.
- o If carefully structured, office-condo conversions open new profit avenues.
- o Especially desirable for stable tenants with minimal expansion/contraction, such as medical office tenants and smaller law firms.
- o New construction costs severely dampen potential oversupply issues.
- o These sites may be eligible for alternative property-type conversion in changing areas near urban core.

Danger Zones

- o Not as sensitive to location as other property types. Tenants flee if rents are more competitive down the street—more of a commodity play for users.

o   Not a critical property type, office users find
lower-priced alternatives such as the home,
industrial flex buildings, and even retail locations
where direct customer contact is required.

o   Office sites are less sensitive to exact site dynamics
(for example, retail center at a main traffic light)
and developing alternative office parks is easy.

o   Technology gains reduced the number of workers
and larger storage space. Hoteling workers pose a
real threat to long-term growth.

o   Current reported vacancy rates are high and rarely
account for the phantom space market overhang.

o   Avoid auto-only destinations, as more workers want
new transportation options.

Plan of Attack

o   Larger-scale downtown investments bode well from
the diversified and expanding service sector.

o   Expect modest profits as this sector is fully-priced.

o   Smaller management-intensive medical office
and professional buildings offer unique niche
opportunities. On-campus preferred and longer-term
ground leases are common, as hospitals control
immediate area development.

Reconnaissance

o   Commercial Real Estate Development Association
and Building Owners and Managers Association/
BOMA International are respected office building
information sources for development, leasing,
building operating costs, energy consumption

patterns, local and national building codes, legislation, occupancy statistics, and technological news.

6. Lodging

"I like being on the road, living in hotels. While I've got a real nice house, I go crazy when I'm there."
Tommy Shaw

Lodging facilities are war chests crowded with visitors. Among the most management-intensive property sectors, lodging continues on a steady upward climb since the Great Recession. Business and tourist travelers are the backbone of this industry. Technological upgrades along with higher levels of internet bookings enable increased profits based on substantial cost savings.

What's hot? Full-service hotels in the key markets and limited-service hotels without food and beverage. Hotel condos are emerging as options for smaller investors. Beware: strong technical expertise and sophisticated investment capabilities required.

Strike Zones

- o Branding flags matter. The higher the quality and recognition of the chain scale, the better the occupancy.
- o Lodging provides the fastest adjustments to cash flows based on daily room rates.
- o Land scarcity and rising construction costs create high barriers to entry.

- o Lodging expansion is underway but on a limited scale with significant risks.
- o Multiple profit sources (theme parks, parking, vending machines) scattered throughout the premises.
- o Resort hotels are highly profitable and equally risky. Extensive amenity packages required.
- o Business and leisure travelers are better served by expanded, luxury facilities including fitness rooms, private mini-gyms, and personal trainers.

Danger Zones

- o More than any other property types, lodging premises are notoriously volatile and highly sensitive to the economy and travel issues.
- o New construction threatens secondary and marginal locations.
- o High energy costs impact personal travel and business appetite.
- o Technologies such as teleconferencing centers reduce in-person meetings.
- o Heavy reliance on third-party management reduces direct control.

Plan of Attack

- o Be cautious. The do-it-yourself operator is vanishing, as a clear separation between management and ownership develops.
- o Lodging offers opportunities to expand products and services as theme facilities become more

commonplace, including water parks and other non-room-related revenue streams.
- o This sector demands agility and requires serving niche markets.
- o The prime targets have been captured. Simple repositioning leaves minor profit margins.
- o Hotel condos are effective timeshare units—ideal for operators but less profitable for owners.

Reconnaissance

- o Travel Industry Association of America. Represents the widest scope of lodging interests.
- o Smith Travel Research. Leader in hotel research and statistics.

7. Miscellaneous

Additional investment opportunities include mixed-use complexes, parking structures, assisted living, skilled care, infrastructure, restaurants, land speculation, service stations, sports facilities, and golf courses. These specialized properties have higher risks and rewards. Some of the distressed assets classified in the four food groups fall into this category, but most are characterized as operating businesses, not realty investments.

Reconnaissance

- o The Urban Land Institute is the best all-around real estate organization and think-tank trade group that covers nearly all sectors of the industry. If looking for a single real estate organization that covers all the bases with a national scope, look no further.

FUTURE TARGETS?

"Design is about making things good (and then better) and right (and fantastic) for the people who use and encounter them."

Matt Beale

As technological and social changes rapidly progress, the boundaries between property types continue to blur. Office, retail, storage, entertainment, and living spaces continue to tightly integrate. War chests are more like live stages. Regularly changing props and scenery are discussed below:

- With online activities such as auctions, a basement doubles as storage space and retail distribution space.
- The picture hanging on the wall serves as a flat screen television set, a stereo, and a computer monitor.
- The desk functions as an office, library, and multimedia entertainment center.
- The yard or farm adds windmill power for extra electricity to be sold to utility companies.
- The living room serves as an exercise gymnasium, meeting area, extended dining room, play area, and convertible guest room.
- The hotel teleconference room functions as a meeting area, lunch room, and convention facility.
- The retail store is a warehouse, distribution center, automobile repair facility, and shopping area (for example, warehouse clubs).

As future generations of combat investors learn to harness and redistribute space more effectively, real estate will change further. March on! The future awaits with new territories and properties to be conquered. The war chests come in all shapes, sizes, and locations.

CHAPTER 7

READY, AIM, FIRE: GAME ON!

"Drive thy business or it will drive thee."
Benjamin Franklin

Battle stations, battle stations! Load your weapons and stand by. Now . . . ready, aim, fire!

READY . . . THE WAR ROOM

You've got your weapons ready, picked a location, and targeted a project in the crosshairs. Your palms are sweating. It's time to start making decisions in the War Room, which could be on your smartphone, PC or laptop in your office or in a café—anywhere you collect and process data, distribute information, and keep track of your battle campaign. Your war chest is empty and ready for a fill up. Your war machine is tuned and ready to go!

Are you ready for investment battle? Attack or wait? Fast or slow? Large scale or small? Aggressive or conservative? Decide whether you want to play in the arena with real money and time or be a sideline spectator. Let's determine how prepared you are for investing commitment by exploring the spectrum of real estate investing battlefronts:

1. **Observation Zone**
    This is the observation gallery and purely for spectators. You're in this zone to learn about targets from various public and private information sources. Zone members include government officials, urban planners, trade associations, students, scholars, media professionals, researchers, and other personnel offering preliminary information or interested in learning more about the industry. No financial risk.

2. **Contact Zone**
    Ready to move out of the observation gallery? Want some target practice? If so, you're entering the contact or prospecting zone. You're in contact with prospective sellers or buyers, but no financial actions are taken yet. Information service providers offer leads and site targets, but the work remains far from the target for months, sometimes years, if at all. You're applying knowledge but still not ready to pull the trigger.

3. **Action Zone**
    You're in the target area with loaded ammunition. No more academia or practice. Sparks are starting to fly in the

action zone. A glimmer of light for the combat investor. And while you've locked on to targets in this zone, you're still uncommitted. This zone is a forward reconnaissance area covered by detailed diligence of the targeted premises. Extensive communications between buyer, broker, and seller determine whether the target is truly worth pursuing. This zone provides income opportunities for consultants and financial advisors.

4. **Transaction Zone**

   The target is a go! You've pulled the trigger and fire! The deal is under contract. All efforts are aimed at closing within the buyer and seller's timelines. At this stage of combat, failure can be a costly mistake, as monies have been spent on detailed due diligence, title and survey, appraisals, environmental/engineering reports, and other services. Once the seller is paid, the buyer holds a new investment. Victory, if you've done your homework right!

AIM . . . FOCUS

"Don't let the mistakes and disappointments of the past control and direct your future."

Zig Ziglar

Now that you know what zones you're prepared to cross, it's time to ask some tough questions about the timing of an action plan. Are market conditions ripe to execute the plan? Is the supply and demand balance right? Are mortgage rates low enough? Are sufficient funds available to carry the project if problems arise? Are the appropriate personnel on the team? Have you assessed and mitigated risks? Are you taking a stab at the investment now or dodging a falling risk knife?

Wouldn't you like to find a leprechaun sitting on the war chest? Perfect timing requires luck, but good timing doesn't. Perfect timing comes on occasion; good timing is planned. Assuming full preparation for attack, when is a good time? It depends how well the game plan is tuned into market cycles, which follow some clear patterns. Since supply and demand fluctuations tied to brick-and-mortar construction (and destruction) are inherently slower paced, the real estate asset class lags other leading economic indicators like stocks and bonds.

Universally speaking, real estate cycles through normal, liberal, and conservative conditions.

- **Normal Cycles**

  "In investing, what is comfortable is rarely profitable."
  Robert Arnott

  Normal market cycles reflect equilibrium in the real estate supply and demand for any given market or property type. The war chest opens and closes without too many problems. Hallmarks of normal cycles include:

  - buzz words ("stable," "regular," "comfortable," "predictable")
  - a reasonable balance of active funding sources (for example, banks, insurance companies, securitized debt, pension fund, and private debt capital)
  - diverse balance of institutional and private buyers, with no specific source leading the market
  - transactions close within normal timelines—typically 90 to 120 days

- vacant land sales more active, auctions less common as few motivated sellers and buyers are in the market
- general performance levels for properties are above break-even, matched by price equilibrium
- public markets return with more income-oriented programs, driving entrepreneurial players to traditional roles of value-add ventures via repositioning, new construction, and rehab.

Phrases signifying that conditions are steady and perhaps some positive change is on the horizon are as follows:

- "We're seeing a runoff in [rent] concessions."
- "Many companies have had lean operations, pushing their productivity limits."
- "This is a good time to look at real estate as a defensive measure, steady cash flow with inflation protection."
- "Not much new construction, only some owner-occupied and build-to-suit ventures."
- "I have very similar mortgage quotes from different sources."
- "It makes sense to build now, as the area needs extra housing."
- "The broker called and said there is only a handful of properties, but more bidders are back."

- **Liberal Cycles**

"The four most expensive words in the English language are: this time it's different."

Sir John Templeton

The war chest stays wide open and unlocked. Otherwise overheated, these cycles reflect supply and demand imbalances favoring new construction with premium pricing.

- replacement cost discussions overtake income and market approach valuation models, as funding sources look to justify new construction
- pro forma underwriting is very common, buying future versus current cash flow
- transactions close quicker, as buyers are very motivated to invest cash, typically 90 days or less
- forward-delivery financing is abundant, as lenders and investors lose deals for existing assets in search of new construction opportunities
- less risk differentiation between various property types and locations as secondary and primary markets are priced nearly equally as office, retail, industrial, and even lodging properties, indicating a price run-up
- merchant builders frequently announce new spec construction projects
- market euphoria causes long-term holders to sell, as the right price is available at ridiculously favorable terms
- high leverage and low capitalization rates supported by record transaction volume
- frequent conversations about the market reaching perfection

Buzzwords and phases of the liberal cycle suggest quick profits, a never-ending positive financial cycle, and easy financing with minimum money down.

- "Don't worry about the cash flow, the property appreciation will go through the roof!"
- "The next guy will certainly pay a higher price!"
- "The deal is already under contract, above the asking price!"
- "I'm moving more money into real estate from stocks and bonds."
- "Everything here has appreciated so quickly."
- "We're not at the top of the market, it's simply a new baseline."
- "Let's start a real estate investment club."
- "Funding sources are crawling over each other to lend me money."
- "Did you attend last week's wealth building seminar? It was packed!"
- "How can you go wrong in real estate!"

- **Conservative Cycles**

"The market does not beat them. They beat themselves because though they have brains, they cannot sit tight."
Jesse Livermore

The war chest seems shut and the lock is jammed. Conservative market conditions spawn predictions of the apocalypse. Headlines spout negative news. Buyers and sellers retreat. Institutional players are sidelined. Chaos and panic prevail in this cycle.

- real estate is a dirty word
- frequent layoffs in construction, architectural, and development firms occur; financial institutions plagued by instability

- property management is back in vogue, as financial engineering and defensive measures protect cash flow
- capital sources try to retreat and exit troubled deals
- extreme price uncertainty and seller denial of declining values exist
- auctions, short sales, and other quick-closing methods gain popularity as funding sources look to dump assets
- increased lawsuits for bankruptcies, foreclosures, tenant cancellation enforcement, and other unpaid fees
- all-cash deals with a real private and public capital resurface; savvy investors return to buy back the properties sold at peak prices

Conservative cycle verbiage is somber and defeatist, with investors complaining about problems rather than opportunities.

- "No one knows the real price, as the property is financially underwater."
- "Motivated seller will consider all offers."
- "In borrowing money, the sponsorship financial net worth and liquidity is more important than ever."
- "Banks are not making loans but selling them instead."
- "The signs on the building say, 'short sale, new price, bank owned, and must sell.'"
- "The appreciation was not what I expected."
- "My broker moved out of state and is living with his family."
- "Hard assets mean hard times."

- "Everyone's scared to bid, as prices may drop further!"
- "*How to Buy Foreclosures* is a popular real estate investing book title."

Beyond the three real estate market cycles discussed above, real estate investors go through personal cycles. Such conditions are tied to the investor issues, often presenting unique opportunities that maybe independent of any of these cycles.

- **Personal Cycles**

   Investors react to triggers related to changing personal needs, unusual circumstances, and unrelated financial issues, including the following:

   - sudden change in portfolio circumstances—a margin call
   - unforeseen ownership issues not necessarily related to individual—partner or corporate financial issues, bankruptcy
   - personal situational change—job relocation, promotion, layoff
   - unique opportunity—next-door neighbor is selling an adjacent property that would substantially enhance the value of your property, even at a premium price
   - winning the lottery!

A savvy game plan tied to the right market and personal investment conditions and a dose of luck propels you to take the final step . . . the closing!

FIRE! CLOSING THE DEAL

"A deal dies several times before closing."
Anonymous Broker Saying

No more deliberating and planning, no more cash flow modeling—it's closing time! Time to cram your war chest with the spoils. By adhering to the "Always Be Closing" law all along, you're prepared. The homework is done and the checklist complete. You've retained a reputable closing attorney and even checked with the police department about any recent crime activity in the area. And you've leveraged off of all professionals involved in the transaction—both directly and indirectly.

Yet be prepared to bail out and jump ship as the ultimate precaution. If the seller refuses to disclose any relevant information, you should turn around and walk away. That is, unless purchasing a "bargain basement" deal, know the risks very well. Always find out what the seller knows that you don't. It'll be too late to bring up these issues at the closing table, unless the seller is prepared to respond accordingly (for example, a discounted price).

The closing process is sometimes unpredictable, chaotic, and costly beyond any original projections. A successful transaction requires incredibly sharp focus throughout the entire closing process. To prevent disaster, you need to be sure your war chest is well protected by using the following procedures:

- Obtain written estimates on closing costs ahead of time to stay on budget and alert all professionals about cost control.
- Always pay brokers, attorneys, appraisers, and your entire team in a timely manner to show respect for their work and secure loyalty.

- Never let your guard down—targets are constantly moving and so should you.

Knowing how to aim and open fire on investments for your war chest leads to understanding pillar purchasing power—the four pillars (4Ps) of a real estate investment fortress.

PILLAR PURCHASING POWER

The 4Ps that uphold the framework of a solid, well-protected fortress for both warfare and real estate investing are people, place, project and performance.

People (an army or investing team) conquer or purchase a new **place** (foreign land or real estate location) to enable a **project** (building an empire or a building) resulting in successful **performance** (maintaining power or control of the project).

Always remember the 4Ps in *all* real estate investing; it's a simple yet effective rule of thumb that applies to any type of premises discussions.

The combat investment philosophy, armed with a slew of weapons and technologies, embodies the importance of territorialism. The philosophy illustrates the spectrum of attack strategies available to the investor. Military equipment is used offensively to gain territory. Even defensive military equipment is designed to disable the opponent. Long-range equipment supports long-range objectives; limited equipment reflects short-term drive.

But as history has proven, not all territorial investment objectives work as planned. Before launching your war machine, let's perform some reconnaissance on historical blunders, successes, and lessons learned for real estate investing.

CHAPTER 8

RECONNAISSANCE: LEARNING FROM PAST VICTORIES AND DEFEATS

"Those who do not learn from history are doomed to repeat it."
George Santayana

Newton's Third Law—to every action there is always an equal and opposite reaction—clearly applies to war where the winner's victory means the loser's defeat. Victories come from lessons learned from defeat. Even in a stalemate conflict, a victor and loser ultimately emerge—it just takes longer and teaches different lessons.

History offers dozens of lessons with both spectacular triumphs and arrogant blunders. Combat investors should heed the warnings of these lessons, namely technology changes, but human nature does not. Mistakes are inevitable. Repeating them is unforgiveable.

RIGHT IDEAS, WRONG PLANS

The past two centuries are filled with military blunders, lessons garnered, new armies, and fronts forged. Glean some valuable lessons from history's military mistakes and avoid dropping the war chest on your foot . . . or worse!

French Invasion of 1812 (echoed by Operation Barbarossa, 1941-1945)

"Nothing is foolproof to a sufficiently talented fool."
Anonymous

Napoleon tried to conquer Russia without fully preparing for sustained operation in an extreme climate. Nazi Germany repeated the mistake a century later. Both were aware of Russia's harsh climate; both led strong armies supported by the best technology of the day. Neither used common sense, however, and both were defeated by Mother Nature and defenders who knew their homeland better than the would-be conquerors.

Real estate investors repeatedly make the same mistakes by journeying into ill-prepared forays within unfamiliar areas. Instead of using optimally-matched resources and contracting local experts, leasing and management teams are cobbled together out of home office staff. This group of losers includes drones, jet fighters, B-52s, aircraft carriers, and occasionally submarines. Bunkers and tanks clean up after them.

Minefield: Inappropriate choice of geography and property type.

The Battle of Little Bighorn, 1876

"An army of asses led by a lion is better than an army of lions led by an ass."

George Washington

In one of the most incompetently planned modern military disasters, General Custer tried to force the Sioux back into reservations. Ignoring orders to wait for the full cavalry support to arrive, he led his limited troops carrying minimal supplies in an attack on hill and ravine terrain that the Sioux knew intimately. Outnumbered three to one, Custer was doomed to failure.

In this scenario, tanks and stealth track as the biggest losers. Sometimes drones lose if not sponsored by substantial capital and personnel at the property level. B-52s take on too many targets. Strategic strike power, adequate capital, and resources are imperative for complicated, obstacle-riddled investments. Subs and carriers hunt comfortably in these waters.

Minefield: Insufficient resources and foolish bravery.

The Verdun Offensive, 1916

"We are not retreating—we are advancing in another direction."

General Douglas MacArthur

The Germans defensively protected one front and attacked another. Rather than pursuing an aggressive strategy, the Germans wore out the French by baiting them into fighting on the front line, then retreating. During this battle campaign, one of the costliest in history, nearly a million soldiers perished on both sides of the battlefield.

In an effort to find ideal deals, investors experiment with popular strategies of the day. Full risk assessments are superseded by the search for yield, seeking to be where the action is. Many investors expand from core assets (fully-leased properties with strong rent rolls) to opportunity assets (requiring more management and leasing risk). These investors fluctuate between operating and developing assets—completely different operations requiring alternative risk profiles and skill sets.

This formula fails because it's neither clearly defensive (core) nor conclusively offensive (development). Jet fighters, B-52 bombers, and aircraft carriers often are guilty of this mistake. Due to direct knowledge of the territory, bunkers and tanks flourish, while stealth's intelligence enables acquisition of the best deals left over from the whole debacle.

Minefield: Indecision and confusing plans.

The Battle of Midway, 1942

"Therefore a victorious army first wins and then seeks battle; a defeated army first battles and then seeks victory."

Sun Tzu

This bloody naval engagement resulted in one of history's most decisive victories. It was the first naval battle in which ships did not engage each other directly. Instead, aircraft rapidly sunk millions of tons of floating armor. Reliable intelligence was converted into swift decisions within a framework of limited resources, producing a sweeping victory. Despite Japan's abundance of ships and aircraft, accurate intelligence enabled the Americans to decode Japanese battle plans and stage a surprise attack. Midway is a striking example of how resourceful talent and strategy overpower superior arms.

Investors learn many lessons from Midway. They assume that capable staffs, ample capital, and strong market presence guarantee victory. But these same investors fail to realize that the hungrier underdogs are forced to take more calculated and bold risks, structuring deals with less contingencies as their buying advantage.

Tanks, carriers, drones, and submarines are usually the victims in this scenario. All others, especially stealth, are the likely victors. Tanks believe they know the market better than any outsiders and refuse to overpay based on historical pricing prejudices. Drones study data more than the actual asset. Carriers and submarines assume sellers will give them carte blanche because of their financial firepower. With good research, the B-52s succeed as part of their carpet bombing buying strategies. And the intelligence-gathering stealth are right on target while helicopters do well by conquering the tougher opportunities.

Minefield: Overconfidence and underestimating the enemy.

The Cold War, 1946-1991

"We didn't win the Cold War, we were just a big bank that bankrupted a smaller bank because we had an arms race that wiped the Russians out."

Norman Mailer

For nearly half a century, two superpowers pointed nuclear warheads at each other. This muscle-flexing contest proved to be the costliest in history—consuming more than half of these superpowers' economies. Military actions by both powers (Korea, Hungary, Cuba, Czechoslovakia, and Vietnam) expanded vast resources. Rather than directly engaging in battle, these superpowers displayed their technical prowess on global battlefronts. The show of arms proved too costly for the Soviet Union because it was an assembly of captive nations unable to gain a productivity advantage.

The Cold War investor issue is a problem of being big and bulky. Large-weapon platforms are usually the victims. In particular, carriers and B-52s do poorly on the investment front. These groups spend too much time on marketing investments and less time on management. Often, they're unable to make quick decisions as operating styles can be more important than changing market conditions. Submarines go either way, depending upon entrepreneurial levels of the ownership. Alternatively, tanks, bunkers, helicopters, drones, stealth, and jet fighters do well because plans change on the dime and resources reallocate accordingly without too many layers of decision-making.

Minefield: Misallocation of resources based on flawed plans with no clear exit strategy.

The Gulf War, 1991

"Those who live by the sword get shot by those who don't."

Anonymous

Coalition forces crushed the Iraqi invasion of Kuwait. Swift movement, superior technology, ample preparation, and a well-organized attack propelled a clear-cut victory. The Iraqi forces were neither prepared nor equipped to respond to the Coalition's air superiority.

In the world of combat investing, technology discussions are less of an issue than in the past. The playing field is more even for gathering market intelligence for making financial decisions. Nearly everyone has access to affordable word processing, database management, and spreadsheet software, as well as the internet. Real estate investing is not an instantly-priced asset class compared to stocks and bonds. Investors have ample time to research markets, overall demographics, capital sources, and pricing trends.

Assuming the combat investor has sufficient resources to execute the business plan, all styles (except the risk-averse bunker) are winners or losers with the Gulf War analogy. In this case, the great differentiator is information interpretation. Two investors review the same information and arrive at totally different financial conclusions. The art of making the deal, not the science.

Minefield: Insufficient resources and technology.

Leaving history's battlefields, let's look to your future as a combat investor.

FUTURE COMBAT INVESTOR?

With the war chest packed in the trunk, the combat investor charges into the future battlefield with a war machine, constantly checking the rearview mirror for lessons of the past. But this combat investor has all of the financial targets locked on with deadly precision. The real estate holdings are smart and more destruction-proof. The combat investor instantly knows everything about the well-protected war chest contents. Little is left to chance. The combat investor's future is here today.

Like predecessors who captured opportunities presented by their environment, tomorrow's combat investors value quality over quantity. More is done with less—regulating security, comfort, lighting, and space reuse. This investor is aware of the following:

- **Population Growth**
  More people use less space, so get used to it. The combat investor will be far more space-savvy with much more emphasis on quality vs. quantity of space.

- **Vertical vs. Horizontal**
  Up, up, and away! You should expect to see less garden apartments and more high-rise units.

- **Urban vs. Suburban**
  Infrastructure maintenance costs, higher energy prices, aging housing stock built with lower quality materials, and a lower-income population base will create more suburban blight. Conversely, inner-city core development will continue to rebound. Look at European cities as good examples as to where American cities are heading. You'll find more wealth closer to the urban core.

- **Inflation**
  Real estate investing continues to benefit from inflationary pressures. In general, as the dollar shrinks, real estate expands.

- **Sustainability**
  Compost, water, and other building systems will be
  self-contained. You need to think of the nuclear submarine
  operating as an independent vessel. In other words,
  tomorrow's real estate is smarter and more self-reliant.

- **Space Exploration**
  The cycle of colonization, industrialization,
  consumerization, and optimization will be repeated in
  outer space. Colonization will conquer foreign planets,
  introducing the galactic combat investor (Star Trek stuff!).

Future combat investors will come in all shapes, sizes, and
ambition levels. Anyone who embodies the required attitude
and willpower is a combat investor. Combat investing is blind to
race, color, and creed. It does not differentiate between college
educated and street smart. No borders, no language barriers, and
no exceptions—just the desire to succeed. The combat investor is a
"land mind" with an insatiable appetite for learning and taking on
new challenges to financially control premises.

Warriors know that territorial gain demands territorial
responsibility. Today's combat investor is not only a business
warrior but a resource manager—a custodian of water, soil, and
air on the premises, a war machine used for constructive, not
destructive purposes.

For the combat investor of the future, the battlefield will serve not
only as a financial war venue but it will be elevated to a treasured
resource preserve. **"RE"** will no longer stand only for "real estate"
but will encompass:

- **RE**cycling
- **RE**configuring
- **RE**plenishing
- **RE**designing
- **RE**positioning
- **RE**distributing
- **RE**formulating
- **RE**prioritizing
- **RE**pricing
- **RE**fining
- **RE**trofitting
- **RE**sizing
- **RE**tooling and a host of other
- **RE**sponsible operations

Now that you're **RE**freshed and ready for action, tap into your landgrabbing instincts to build your war chest of real estate treasures. With your new warfare attitude, you're a war machine on the territorial attack—a realty war machine . . . a tank, bomber, jet fighter, or submarine!

Search and invade your targets. Take financial control of your premises. You're now a combat investor! Forward march!

ABOUT THE AUTHOR

John Oharenko is a veteran real estate financier, investor, author, and lecturer. Over his thirty-year career, John financed in excess of three billion dollars of various types of income-producing real estate including apartments, industrial, retail, office, hospitality, and land ventures. He also personally invests in multifamily and commercial properties.

John authored three books and over one hundred articles on real estate investing and Chicago history. He lectures nationally on real estate investing and has been quoted by the *Wall Street Journal*, *Journal of Property Management*, *Appraisal Journal*, *Chicago Tribune* and the *Los Angeles Times*. John is a founding member of the Real Estate Capital Institute and an active member of the Urban Land Institute.

John holds a master's degree in real estate appraisal and investment analysis from the University of Wisconsin-Madison and an undergraduate degree in business from DePaul University.

John's childhood experiences growing up in Chicago's Humboldt Park, military school, and martial arts training have greatly influenced his investment philosophy.

ACKNOWLEDGEMENTS

"O Lord my God, I will give thanks to Thee forever."
Bible, Psalms 30:12

I'm very grateful to my family and friends who've supported me—socially, academically, and professionally.

My late parents, Vladimir and Lubomyra Oharenko, gave me discipline, sent me to military school to refine my life skills, and always encouraged my entrepreneurial spirit.

Professors Mike Farrell of DePaul University and Dr. James Graaskamp inspired me to learn about real estate investing and guided me through my formative college years.

Grandmaster Gary Keller and others in the martial arts community taught me the value of understanding self-defense and how to stay physically and spiritually balanced.

My various employers and business partners who helped mold my professional real estate career include Baird & Warner, Cushman & Wakefield, GMAC Commercial Mortgage Corporation, Capmark, and Berkadia.

Special thanks to the people who've helped me write this book, including Maria Oharenko, Oryna Schiffman and Lorraine Fico-White.

Select images provided by iStockphoto, Military Vizualizations Inc., Pond5, PresenterMedia and Stocksnapper. All rights reserved.

John Oharenko

COMBAT GEAR

The Logo
The circle in the combat investor logo represents the earth (real estate) with the green color signifying money. The percent sign integrated into the dollar sign illustrates the dynamics between profit (yield) and funds invested (principal)—the yin and yang of investing.

The Helmet
The combat investor helmet symbolizes the durability and persistence of military discipline, uniformity, respect, and battle-readiness. The combat investor is willing to instantly attack emerging opportunities. The one-size-fits-all helmet is available to all investors who venture to apply their personal style, investment goals, and objectives to combat investing.

The Uniform
Though the combat investor doesn't have a dress code, an attitude of confidence and competence is always projected.